JUST
PEACEMAKERS

JUST PEACEMAKERS

An Introduction to Peace and Justice

Mary Evelyn Jegen, SND de N

Paulist Press
New York/Mahwah, N.J.

Cover and book design by Lynn Else
Copyright © 2006 by Sisters of Notre Dame de Namur, Ohio Province

Library of Congress Cataloging-in-Publication Data

Jegen, Mary Evelyn.
Just peacemakers : an introduction to peace and justice / Mary Evelyn Jegen.
    p. cm.
ISBN 0-8091-4350-X (alk paper)
1. Christianity and justice—Catholic Church. 2. Nonviolence—Religious aspects—Catholic Church. 3. Christian sociology—Catholic Church. I. Title.
BX1795.J87J44 2005
261.8'73—dc22

                                                                2005017818

Published by Paulist Press
997 Macarthur Boulevard
Mahwah, New Jersey 07430

www.paulistpress.com

Printed and bound in the
United States of America

Contents

To Pax Christi International,
since 1945 witnessing to the peace of Christ
through prayer, study, and action

Acknowledgments

I thank with all my heart the Sisters of Notre Dame, particularly the local communities of Mount Notre Dame, Cincinnati, and St. Robert Bellarmine, Chicago, who were an unfailing support during the writing of this book. I am very grateful to Sister Elizabeth Marie Bowyer for reading the manuscript, to Sister Angela Franks for her careful proofreading, and to my sisters, Carol Frances Jegen, BVM, and Evelyn Jegen, RC, for their constant encouragement. Many former students and friends, far too many to mention by name, helped shape this book. I am especially grateful to Sister Mary Ann Cook, SND, Sister Edith Ryan, SND, Ruth Druhan, Margareta Ingelstam, and Jan and Martin Benton. Finally, I thank the staff of Paulist Press, especially Father Lawrence Boadt and Paul McMahon for wise advice at an early stage of this book, and Nancy de Flon for her skillful editing.

Introduction

Just Peacemakers draws on long years of teaching and learning with adults in both academic and informal settings. During these years I have also been involved in national and international peace and justice movements and organizations, always inspired and sustained by companions on the journey. From these experiences as both teacher and activist, I am convinced of the importance of effective methods of understanding and action on issues that call for our response. Above all, we need the companionship of others in prayer, study, reflection, and action. This in turn gives the energy and enthusiasm that makes action for justice and peace and for the transformation of the world a joyful experience of Christian ministry. All of us who long for justice and peace probably feel overwhelmed, at least occasionally, by the sheer enormity of the social problems crying for our attention. This book aims to provide resources for just such a situation.

The first two chapters look at characteristics of Jesus and at our call to discipleship. This is the foundation of our action on behalf of justice and peace. Chapters 3 and 4 consider a Christian theology of active nonviolence and ways in which nonviolence is practiced. Chapters 5 and 6 deal with effective methods of learning and with ways of personal growth in work for justice and peace. Chapters 7 and 8 deal with the multiple contexts in which we are called to work and with some of the profound changes in our culture that impact our efforts.

The final two chapters, 9 and 10, examine personal and group ways of working for social change and look at a number of organized peace and justice movements. These organizations and movements enable us to work effectively with others, doing together what we could never do alone. The questions at the end of each chapter may be useful for personal study and reflection and also for conversation and discussion.

CHAPTER ONE

— ❖ —

Church:
A Community of Disciples

You show me the path of life. In your presence
there is fullness of joy.
—Psalm 16:11

CHAPTER FOCUS

At the heart of our Christian life is a vocation to a community of disciples we call the church. Disciples learn from close association with Jesus, who is characterized by intimacy with God and inexhaustible, unrestricted compassion for people. Discipleship has social implications: we are called to respond to human needs and to love our enemies. We approach social issues within the mystery of our vocation to share God's love and ongoing work of creative redemption.

Way of Discipleship

How should we Christians see ourselves in society? What should be our distinctive mark? Simply, Christians are to see themselves as a community of disciples of Jesus. While this has been true from the beginning of Christianity, in our time the significance of discipleship has been brought into clear relief in Catholic social teaching and related theological works.[1]

To love as Jesus loved us is possible to the extent that we follow the way of Jesus with the freedom and joy of close companionship, of friendship. This is what is at the heart of discipleship. The word *discipleship* is not in common usage today outside of a religious context, so it is worthwhile to reflect on its original meaning. *Disciple*, related to the word *discipline*, has to do with learning by doing, in close relationship with a master teacher. *Apprentice* comes close to the notion of disciple, but *apprenticeship* does not include the idea of sharing a master teacher's way of life. An apprentice learns a craft or skill; a disciple learns a way of living. This sharing of a way of life is essential to discipleship.

Our discipleship is both personal and communal. Jesus formed a group of disciples from those he called one by one. It is clear from the gospel accounts that Jesus put great store in the formation of his community of disciples. His teaching was both difficult to understand and radically different from any other body of learning or practical skill his disciples had known. Disciples of Jesus were called to something far deeper than external imitation. They were, in Jesus' own words, to be filled with the Holy Spirit, whom he would send to be their advocate and their strength (John 14:16–17, 26). Jesus' disciples were to live in him, and he would live in them in a way unlike anything they had ever experienced. Not until after his death and resurrection did they understand the depth of his teaching.

The disciples exhibited serious shortcomings and character flaws, and some of these traits they carried to their graves. At the time of Jesus' final crisis, one of the Twelve Apostles betrayed him, another denied that he knew him, and the rest abandoned him. This, however, was not the end of the story. Through the power of the Holy Spirit, these same men became faithful disciples and took on the characteristics of Jesus, even to laying down their lives as he had given his own life.

Intimacy with God

According to Monika Hellwig, the two characteristics of Jesus that were most central to his experience were "intimacy with God and inexhaustible, non-exclusive compassion for people."[2] Jesus experienced his intimacy with God through his relationships with people as well as in prayer, and he consistently sought times and places for prayerful communion with God. When the disciples asked him to teach them how to pray, he taught them to call God "Abba," that is, "Father," using a most affectionate term for parent. Jesus' intimacy with God was more than that of a contemplative person or a great mystic. His enemies charged him with claiming to be the Son of God, and he went to his death charged with this claim. An early Christian hymn in the Letter of Saint Paul to the Philippians speaks of this mystery:

> Let the same mind be in you that was in Christ Jesus,
> who, though he was in the form of God,
> > did not regard equality with God
> > as something to be exploited,
> but emptied himself,
> > taking the form of a slave,
> > being born in human likeness.
> And being found in human form,
> > he humbled himself
> > and became obedient to the point of death—
> > even death on a cross.
>
> Therefore God also highly exalted him
> > and gave him the name
> > that is above every name,
> so that at the name of Jesus
> > every knee should bend,
> > in heaven and on earth and under the earth,
> and every tongue should confess
> > that Jesus Christ is Lord,
> > to the glory of God the Father. (Phil 2:5–11)

Jesus' intimacy with God gave him a vision, which he called the kingdom of God, or the reign of God. We are not to understand this as analogous to any earthly kingdom or reign. The expressions "kingdom" or "reign of God" suggest to us earthly regal or authoritarian rule that is largely rejected today. For Jesus, the kingdom or reign of God signifies God acting in human affairs through the liberty of men and women working for the good of all.

Nonexclusive, Inexhaustible Compassion

Next to his intimacy with God, the other salient characteristic of Jesus was his nonexclusive, inexhaustible compassion for people—precisely the quality that upset the status quo. Jesus told a dangerous story about a good Samaritan who helped a wounded man who had been refused aid by religious leaders. They passed the man by rather than go against religious and social taboos (Luke 10:29–37). He told a story of God as a parent with inexhaustible love for a selfish son who squandered his inheritance and came back when he was in desperate need, ready to declare himself unworthy to be called a son but hoping to be accepted as a hired servant. The father responded by killing the fatted calf and throwing a lavish party of welcome because his lost son had been restored to a father's love and home (Luke 15:11–32). The four Gospels show us Jesus consistently reaching out to poor people, outcasts, the sick, and victims of discrimination. In contemporary theological terms, we can say that Jesus was making a preferential and fundamental option for the oppressed poor. The entire Jewish people were subject to the Romans, and one of the realities that Jesus struggled against was the internalizing of their oppression. As a conquered people, the Jews had learned to adjust to their oppressors' agenda, and for many this simply seemed inevitable, because many in leadership positions were in collusion with their oppressors, whether or not they would have described it this way. Jesus worked tirelessly to empower his people to claim their dignity as children of God.

It was especially in the way that he faced the personal crisis caused by his life and teaching that Jesus showed the path his disciples were to follow. With eyes open, he walked into the trap set for him and went to a cruel execution by the torture of the cross, praying for his enemies who, he said, did not really understand what they were doing. This is the mystery of unconditional love that is at the heart of discipleship, and that has kept the community of disciples in existence beyond the life and death of Jesus until the present day. We proclaim in our celebration of the Eucharist, "Dying, you destroyed our death; rising, you restored our life." The glory of God in this world is the cross of his son, Jesus Christ. This is the foolishness of God that is wiser than human wisdom, and the weakness of God that is stronger than human strength (1 Cor 1:25).

Four Characteristics of Disciples

Among the characteristics of Christian discipleship, four are the foundation for all the others. First, *we are called*. Pope John Paul II wrote clearly about this in his first encyclical, *Redeemer of the Human Race:*

> In presenting the complete picture of the People of God...the Second Vatican Council did not deduce this picture merely from a sociological premise....For the whole of the community of the People of God and for each member of it what is in question is not just a specific "social membership"; rather, for each and every one what is essential is a particular "vocation."...Membership in that body has for its source a particular call, united with the saving action of grace. Therefore, if we wish to keep in mind this community of the People of God, which is so vast and so extremely differentiated, we must see first and foremost Christ saying in a way to each member of the community: "Follow me."[3]

The U.S. bishops highlight the theology of "particular call" or vocation in their landmark pastoral letter on peace (1983) and develop it also in their pastoral letter on the U.S. economy (1986). In both cases, their purpose is to ground social action in Christian faith.

Second, to be a disciple means to *take on the mind and heart of Christ, and the consequences that flow from this.* "Come to me, all you that are weary and are carrying heavy burdens, and I will give you rest. Take my yoke upon you, and learn from me; for I am gentle and humble in heart; and you will find rest for your souls. For my yoke is easy, and my burden is light" (Matt 11:28–30). This clarifies why Mary is called the first disciple of Jesus. More than anyone, Mary penetrated to the heart of Jesus' life. In several key episodes of the Gospel, Luke says that Mary kept all that she experienced of Jesus in her heart and pondered its meaning (Luke 2:19, 51). Where others took to their heels when discipleship became dangerous, she was the faithful witness to the end. She models for us a life of loving reflection.

Sandra Schneiders, writing on the Gospel of John, explains the kind of knowledge that characterizes discipleship:

> Th... ....   Jesus that the disciple gradually
> fore, primarily intellectual or infor-
> d of knowledge one has of a friend
> /e know each other intimately." It is,
> aring of life with Jesus. And sharing
> rticipation in the life of God. This
> comes not by way of expiatory sac-
> y suffering by Jesus for us but by
> saved, in John, is not to be rescued
> is included) so much as to be born
> esus dies, John says that he is glo-
> ry being as God's love incarnate is
> se with eyes to see. Revelation
> : expression and full efficacy in
> irough his laying down of his life
>) he is and the active acceptance
> life by the representative disci-
> ...ss, the mother of Jesus and the
> beloved Disciple.[4]

Third, while discipleship is rooted in sharing the inner dispositions of Jesus, *this taking on of his values, that is, of his mind and heart, has external consequences.* It is an historical fact, verified in our own day, that close disciples of Jesus will often find themselves in opposition to much that is considered conventional wisdom and socially acceptable behavior. This was true during the life of Jesus, and it is true for his disciples. Not all will be martyrs, who are the clearest witnesses to the cost of discipleship, but all faithful disciples make costly choices.

Fourth, the entire life of *discipleship finds its meaning in the mystery of love.* Jesus' intimacy with God and his inexhaustible, nonexclusive compassion for people are expressions of one and the same love. An error that bedevils Christian history is the notion that love as Jesus lived it is an ideal that should be kept in view, but that this love cannot be the guiding principle when the cost of loving becomes too high.

The single most important test case is Jesus' clear teaching by word and example that we are to love our enemies. While many Christians, and others, struggle to follow the teaching on love of enemies on the interpersonal level, the teaching to love enemies has historically been put in brackets when applied to enemies, personal or national, who threaten our lives. Yet love of enemies, whether on the personal level or on the societal level, is the acid test of discipleship. This is one of the most difficult social issues facing not only Christians, but the entire human race at this moment in history. To secure our way of life, the government of the United States of America has created a military "security system" based on killing power that has no match. This fact calls us to ponder more deeply the meaning of love of enemies and to collaborate with others in the effort to devise alternatives to war.

Our discipleship, like Mary's, is a personal and ongoing call from God to intimacy with Jesus Christ in his ongoing work of redemption of the world. A single sentence in the document *Justice in the World,* produced by the Roman Synod of 1971, captures the way of discipleship: "The Christian lives under the interior law of liberty, which is a continuing call to man [the person] to turn away from self-sufficiency to confidence in God and from concern for self to a sincere love of neighbor. Thus takes place his [one's] genuine liberation and the gift of self for the freedom of others."[5]

The Acts of the Apostles gives two descriptions of the first communities of disciples. These passages are clearly meant to convey characteristics of a Christian community at any time and place.

> They devoted themselves to the apostles' teaching and fellowship, to the breaking of bread and the prayers. Awe came upon everyone, because many wonders and signs were being done by the apostles. All who believed were together and had all things in common; they would sell their possessions and goods and distribute the proceeds to all, as any had need. Day by day, as they spent much time together in the temple, they broke bread at home and ate their food with glad and generous hearts, praising God and having the goodwill of all the people. And day by day

the Lord added to their number those who were being saved. (Acts 2:42–47)

Now the whole group of those who believed were of one heart and soul, and no one claimed private ownership of any possessions, but everything they owned was held in common. With great power the apostles gave their testimony to the resurrection of the Lord Jesus, and great grace was upon them all. There was not a needy person among them, for as many as owned lands or houses sold them and brought the proceeds of what was sold. They laid it at the apostles' feet, and it was distributed to each as any had need. (Acts 4:32–35)

Four practices are mentioned in these descriptions: breaking bread together, receiving instruction from the apostles, praying together, and sharing goods according to each one's need. Each of these has its contemporary expression as a characteristic of a community of disciples of Jesus. Sharing goods according to each one's needs is a particular challenge for those of us who live in affluent societies in a world characterized by a growing gap between those who are comfortable and the desperate poor. As Gandhi rightly claimed, there was enough in the world for everyone's need, but not for everyone's greed. Catholic social encyclicals have consistently taught that the goods of the world are destined for all and that we are stewards, not absolute owners, of what we call our "property." Fundamentally, all property is held in trust. As Pope John Paul II said so simply in the encyclical *On the Hundredth Anniversary of Rerum Novarum*, immediately following the passage in which he decried war, "Furthermore, it must not be forgotten that at the root of war there are usually real and serious grievances; injustices suffered, legitimate aspirations frustrated, poverty, and the exploitation of multitudes of desperate people who see no real possibility of improving their lot by peaceful means."[6]

In earlier eras, all kinds of ills, physical as well as social, were accepted in a fatalistic way. Today we know that it is possible to change situations that demean human dignity and that cause unnecessary suffering and early death. At the same time, we know that we are not facing the ordinary kinds of problems that we tackle with some efficiency on a day-to-day basis. To get a handle on what we are talking about here, we need to probe more deeply the meaning of a life of discipleship.

Problem and Mystery

Many years ago I saw a poster with a fascinating quotation: "Life is not a problem to be solved but a mystery to be lived." While the words expressed an important truth, at the same time they seemed to me somehow inaccurate. Problem and mystery are both dimensions of life, but they are not in an either/or relationship. I have come to the conclusion that life is a problem, indeed a host of problems, *within* a mystery to be lived. When we locate our problems within the mystery, we have the right relationship between problem and mystery. This is critically important in addressing issues of justice and peace in our time. Let us consider the hard case of war. The twentieth century will go down in history as the century of total war. We are all affected by the past century's dreadful bloodletting on a massive scale. There are connections between wars of the twentieth century, the ongoing intrastate wars today, and the terrorist attacks on September 11, 2001. This presents us with an unsettling array of problems. The cultural impact of violence on all people is immeasurable. Increasingly, we are becoming convinced that war ought not be, while at the same time recognizing that by and large the world still depends on war to put an end to war. We seem to be on the edge of recognizing that war is not merely a problem to be solved, but an expression of a mystery to be faced, and we are not adept at dealing with mystery, or even of describing what we mean by the term.

An equally great tragedy of our time is the destruction of human beings through all that we include in the term *poverty*. More children died in the twentieth century from hunger and malnutrition than from war. In some cases desperate poverty is a cause of war, in other cases an effect. Frequently, hunger is not attributable to lack of food but is a consequence of poverty rooted in unjust social and economic structures. To those who die of poverty, the precise cause hardly matters, but it matters to us. We will not accept poverty as inevitable on anything like the present scale. Science and technology have played a part in engendering the conviction that massive poverty can be overcome. What was once accepted as in the nature of things is now experienced as a human moral challenge.

Nor do we accept war any longer as inevitable, though as a human race we have less of a grasp on alternatives to the violence of war than we have on alternatives to the violence of dehumanizing poverty. A widespread psychic numbing coexists with this revolution of rising expectations, which is related to a penchant for treating social issues as problems to be solved without regard to the dimension of mystery in which they are embedded. As a consequence, many experience emotional and mental fatigue when week after week and year after year they face the same hurdles that seem insurmountable. Those who work for peace and justice wisely find times of withdrawal from active involvement in order to enter into the mystery in which we can best meet the problems that constitute our agenda. There, and only there, do we discover that peace and justice are first of all gifts before they can be the object of our endeavors. The best thing we can do is dispose ourselves to receive these gifts and to share them with others.

Thanks and Praise

When we focus on the Christian mystery in which we live, our spontaneous response is thanks and praise and the desire to share and to celebrate with others. Christian social action flows from thanksgiving when we are aware that we live by gifts—gifts of mind and heart and also material gifts that are the fruit of the earth and the work of human hands. Our very identity is a gift, and the heart of that gift is the capacity for intimacy with God. Ours is to recognize and relish that gift. When we do, joyful thanks and praise are the natural consequence. This is the basic posture for peacemakers.

To see this verified in history, we can begin with the Acts of the Apostles. There we catch something of the joy, energy, and enthusiasm of those who first spread the good news of the new life that was theirs and was meant for all through the life, death, and resurrection of the Lord Jesus. We have not customarily thought of the activity of the earliest Christians as peacemaking, yet it was precisely that. Peace is a keynote of Jesus' passion, death, and resurrection. His own peace was the gift to his own disciples on the night before he died (John 14:27), and his gift on Easter evening when he appeared to them (John 20:19–21). Though the account of the early Christians in Acts includes serious problems that threatened the very existence of the community, the overriding impression is that the sense of mission and of God's gift of the empowering Spirit kept the problems in perspective. Even suffering was something to rejoice in, because it brought the disciples into closer conformity to their risen Lord. Throughout the history of the church, the followers of Jesus witness to this same joy, a word found over and over in the New Testament. Along with peace and love, joy is numbered high among the fruits of the Holy Spirit (Gal 5:22).

Gratitude, or thanks, is a joyful response to a gift received. We talk about a heart welling up with gratitude, an emotion that cannot be contained and calls out for an expression of praise for the giver. In a gift we recognize love and the desire of love for deepening a relationship between giver and receiver. This is true of gifts that spring from personal decision, not of gifts of social convention or those promoted by commercialism. In thanking for a gift, we are really thanking for the love of the giver more than for the gift of the lover. We can learn much from the way very small children react to gifts. Their first response is much more to the gift than to the giver. If the gift is pleasing, the child will express spontaneous delight, but will have to be taught to say "Thank you." We live by gifts, and as we mature we grow in gratitude as we recognize the love of the giver and experience the truth that relationships mean more to us than things.

Matthew's Gospel gives us a picture of Jesus' prayer of thanks and praise during his public ministry. The term *children* in the following passage does not mean those who are not yet adults, but rather those who do not put too high a premium on human achievement and are therefore in tune with the mysterious depth dimension of life.

> At that time Jesus said, "I thank you, Father, Lord of heaven and earth, because you have hidden these things from the wise and the intelligent and have revealed them to infants; yes, Father, for such was your gracious will. All things have been handed over to me by my Father; and no

one knows the Son except the Father, and no one knows the Father except the Son and anyone to whom the Son chooses to reveal him." (Matt 11:25–27)

Immediately after these words Jesus gives the familiar invitation that shows his compassionate recognition of the burdens of discipleship and also the source of strength that comes only from a life of intimacy in which Jesus and the disciple work together. "Come to me, all you that are weary and are carrying heavy burdens, and I will give you rest. Take my yoke upon you, and learn from me; for I am gentle and humble in heart; and you will find rest for your souls. For my yoke is easy, and my burden is light" (Matt 11:28–30).

This mystery of discipleship is an alternative to the problem-solving mentality characteristic of many peace and justice efforts. Jesus did not deny the problems and injustices of his environment, nor was he spared the high price of a prophetic vocation. His labors for the reign of God cost Jesus his life. Yet enshrined in the New Testament as instruction for all subsequent generations of Jesus' disciples is Jesus' declaration that his burden is light because it is the gift of sharing the life and mission of God become one of us. Included in this gift is all the beauty of creation that we see all around us, crowned by the beauty of the human person, marred and wounded but capable of being brought back to the freedom of the children of God. This is symbolized by the heavenly banquet in which God is host in a way that turns conventional expectations upside down.

> Be dressed for action and have your lamps lit; be like those who are waiting for their master to return from the wedding banquet, so that they may open the door for him as soon as he comes and knocks. Blessed are those slaves whom the master finds alert when he comes; truly I tell you, he will fasten his belt and have them sit down to eat, and he will come and serve them. If he comes during the middle of the night, or near dawn, and finds them so, blessed are those slaves. (Luke 12:35–38)

Especially in the Gospel of John do we see the primacy Jesus gave to the mystery of God's desire for us. This is expressed in

Jesus' prayer at the Last Supper with his disciples: "I ask not only on behalf of these, but also on behalf of those who will believe in me through their word, that they may all be one. As you, Father, are in me and I am in you, may they also be in us, so that the world may believe that you have sent me" (John 17:20–21).

These brief reflections on the words and actions of Jesus give us hints of how crucial it is to locate our work for justice and peace within the great mysteries of our faith: creation and redemption. To experience our action for justice and peace as an expression of our incorporation in the life, death, and resurrection of Jesus is to have access to a fountain of living water and the bread of life.

Saint Ignatius, bishop of Antioch who died about 107, once wrote that peace puts an end to every war.[7] Do we believe that? Certainly our culture sees it in just the opposite way, using war as a means to make peace, even though reluctantly. War is seen as a necessary evil. If, as Christians, we are to be countercultural in this matter, holding that war is an unnecessary evil, then it is worth teasing out the meaning of Ignatius's saying that peace puts an end to every war. He means that peace is a gift and a mystery, and that war is a problem to be displaced by peace. This, I believe, is a frontier and new horizon of Christian peacemaking.

We learn to receive and relish the gift of peace by evoking and welcoming others' gifts of mind and heart. Living by shared gifts does not eliminate rigorous social analysis that faces coura-geously the enormity of the injustices and violence that plague our world. But if we are to avoid being overwhelmed by what we face, we do well to remember Ignatius's words about the rela-tionship between peace and war. Peacemaking as task flows from peace as gift.

The peace that is Jesus' gift is the opposite of fear. This is most significant, because while injustice is at the root of war, it is also true that at the root of injustice are not only greed and self-ishness but also fear, fear of a life that would depend fundamen-tally on the quality of relationships rather than on things. "A king is not saved by his great army; a warrior is not delivered by his great strength" (Ps 33:16). Some put their trust in modern armies, and they cannot save either. When social action springs from zeal and enthusiasm to share the good news that peace is fundamen-tally a gift, a way of relating that is constructed day by day, peacemaking efforts and labors for justice grow by attracting others to a genuine peace movement.

QUESTIONS FOR STUDY, REFLECTION, AND CONVERSATION

1. Do you ordinarily think of yourself as a disciple of Jesus? Do you ordinarily think of the church as a community of disciples of Jesus?

2. Intimacy with God characterized Jesus. How do you experience intimacy with God? What are its consequences?

3. "The glory of God in this world is the cross of his son" (p. 4). How do you understand this? Does the passage by Sandra Schneiders (p. 6) help?

4. Do you understand your Christian life as a vocation? What difference does it make?

5. What does it mean that "love of enemies is the acid test of discipleship whether on the personal level or on the societal level"?

6. Does this chapter help you understand why action for justice and peace receives such emphasis today in Catholic social teaching? What factors have contributed to this?

7. How do you understand the saying of Saint Ignatius of Antioch, "Peace puts an end to every war"?

8. Does the explanation of the relationship between problems and mystery give you fresh insight? Motivation? Practical help? Give examples.

NOTES

1. For example, John Paul II, *Redemptor Hominis* (Milan: Editrice Ancora, 1979); Bishops of the United States' pastoral letter on peace (1983) and the U.S. economy (1986); Avery Dulles, SJ, *A Church to Believe In: Discipleship and the Dynamics of Freedom* (New York: Crossroad, 1982); Avery Dulles, SJ, *The Reshaping of Catholicism: Current Challenges in the Theology of Church* (San Francisco: Harper and Row, 1988); Jon Sobrino, SJ, *Christology at the Crossroads* (Maryknoll, NY: Orbis, 1978).

2. Monika K. Hellwig, *Jesus the Compassion of God: New Perspectives on the Tradition of Christianity* (Wilmington, DE: Michael Glazier, 1983), 151.

3. John Paul II, *Redemptor Hominis,* art. 21.

4. Sandra M. Schneiders, *Written That You May Believe: Encountering Jesus in the Fourth Gospel* (New York: Crossroad, 1999), 53. The author has the following note on this passage, including a reference to another helpful source: "John does not deny the sacrificial theology that had become the 'mainstream' theology of the paschal mystery by the time this Gospel was written. But it is clear that he prefers his revelational theology of salvation. A full-scale treatment of this subject is J. Terence Forestell, *The Word of the Cross: Salvation as Revelation in the Fourth Gospel, Analecta Biblica* 57 (Rome: Biblical Institute Press, 1974)."

5. David J. O'Brien and Thomas A. Shannon, eds., *Catholic Social Thought: The Documentary Heritage* (Maryknoll, NY: Orbis, 1992), 289.

6. Ibid., art. 52, p. 478.

7. "Peace is a precious thing: it puts an end to every war waged by heavenly or earthly enemies." Saint Ignatius of Antioch, *Epistle to the Ephesians,* in James A. Kleist, SJ, trans., *The Epistles of St. Clement of Rome and St. Ignatius of Antioch* (Westminster, MD: Newman Press, 1949), 65.

CHAPTER TWO

— ⚜ —

Doing the Truth in Love

*Abide in me, as I abide in you. Just as the branch cannot
bear fruit by itself unless it abides in the vine, neither can
you unless you abide in me.*
—John 15:4

CHAPTER FOCUS

The Eucharist is the central sacrament of the community of
disciples. In it we experience God both nourishing us with the
body and blood of Christ and calling us to live in the new covenant
that Jesus established by his passion, death, and resurrection. The
integrity of the Eucharist requires that we respond to the needs of
others. To live the Eucharist, we need to take time for meditative
prayer on a regular basis. Growth in a eucharistic spirituality will
lead to creative ways of responding to human needs.

Eucharist and Social Action

The word *eucharist* comes from the Greek meaning "thanks"
and "gratitude," and recalls the Jewish blessings that proclaimed
God's works of creation and redemption. The Christian Eucharist
is also called the Lord's Supper, the Breaking of the Bread, Holy
Mass, Holy Communion, and the Blessed Sacrament. No one
name can adequately describe this great mystery.[1]

The Eucharist is the summit and source of the Christian life.
In celebrating the Eucharist, we thank God for everything in our
experience of God's love, not only our personal experience, but
that of the entire human family. The Eucharist is as close as we can

16

come to satisfying our desire to make a return to God for all that God has given to us.

We live by an exchange of gifts. The same God who nourishes us with his body and blood in the Eucharist meets us in poor, sick, and suffering people. Mother Teresa of Calcutta said it well: "The same God who feeds us hungers for us." When the crowd that had been miraculously fed with loaves and fish came to Jesus, he told them clearly that he wanted to give them himself as the very food of life. "I am the bread of life. Your ancestors ate the manna in the wilderness, and they died. This is the bread that comes down from heaven, so that one may eat of it and not die. I am the living bread that came down from heaven. Whoever eats of this bread will live forever; and the bread that I will give for the life of the world is my body" (John 6:48–51).

Why did Jesus choose bread as the symbol of his union with us? Why not fire, which gives warmth and light from the sun, the source of all our earthly energy? The church does use fire as a symbol of Christ himself, especially in the lighting of the paschal candle, which we relight at special sacramental times all during the year. During the sacrament of baptism and again at the rite of Christian burial, the lighted paschal candle is a powerful reminder of Our Lord Jesus Christ. But Jesus did not choose fire for the central sacrament, although he calls himself light in John's Gospel. He chose bread and wine, ordinary foods, to be the primary sacrament of our Christian life. The Eucharist is a sign that says what it does and does what it says: Jesus Christ nourishes our life. Without him we die.

The same Jesus who feeds us hungers for us, and as he satisfies our deepest hunger with himself, so we are called to satisfy his deepest hunger in the way we relate to our brothers and sisters in a love that serves, that hungers and thirsts for justice and commits to being peacemakers. Gandhi said that if God were to appear again on Earth, most certainly he would appear in the form of bread, because it is the only form in which the poor can recognize him.

For Mother Teresa, the sure sign of a vocation to her community was a novice's experienced connection between the body of Christ and the bodies of destitute poor people, especially the sick and dying persons the sisters serve. It is one thing to be able to repeat the words of Jesus, "For I was hungry and you gave me food, I was thirsty and you gave me something to drink, I was a stranger and you welcomed me" (Matt 25:35); it is another thing to act them out in service with a faith recognition that Jesus who is present in the Eucharist under the appearance of bread and wine is as really present in those we meet in our daily lives.

Scripture scholar John Donahue, SJ, tells of trying to explain the theology of the Eucharist to a young Muslim student who had a hard time trying to understand what Catholics believe about the real presence. Finally the student asked, "Well, if they really believed they were receiving the body and blood of Christ together on Sunday, would they treat each other the way they do?"[2]

I remember how Father Pedro Arrupe, superior general of the Jesuits, raised the same question during a homily at the Eucharistic Congress in Philadelphia in 1975. The memory has haunted me for more than a quarter of a century. Father Arrupe said that the integrity of the eucharistic celebration depends fundamentally on how we who celebrate the sacred mystery of Christ's body and blood respond to the needs of his brothers and sisters around the world. The ability to satisfy many hungers of the human family—at least, the physical hungers—is within the power of those of us who are not hungry, if we are willing to do what is necessary. What is necessary goes far beyond alms, although it does not dispense with alms.

In his letter to the church at Corinth, Saint Paul said as much in the terms of his own culture. The physical setting differed from ours, but the heart of the matter is the same. Having become aware of a class division in the very context of the Eucharist, Paul wrote:

> When you come together, it is not really to eat the Lord's supper. For when the time comes to eat, each of you goes ahead with your own supper, and one goes hungry and another becomes drunk. What! Do you not have homes to eat and drink in? Or do you show contempt for the church of God and humiliate those who have nothing? What should I say to you? Should I commend you? In this matter I do not commend you!
>
> For I received from the Lord what I also handed on to you, that the Lord Jesus on the night when he was betrayed took a loaf of bread, and when he had given

thanks, he broke it and said, "This is my body that is for you. Do this in remembrance of me." In the same way, he took the cup also, after supper, saying, "This cup is the new covenant in my blood. Do this, as often as you drink it, in remembrance of me." For as often as you eat this bread and drink the cup, you proclaim the Lord's death until he comes. (1 Cor 11:20–26)

Paul does not leave it to his readers to draw their own conclusion. He tells them, "Whoever, therefore, eats the bread or drinks the cup of the Lord in an unworthy manner will be answerable for the body and blood of the Lord" (1 Cor 11:27).

We desire to celebrate the Eucharist worthily, and that means that we want to make the connection between Jesus present in the eucharistic bread and wine and Jesus present in each person. Gandhi, Mother Teresa, Father Arrupe, the young Muslim student all understood what Jesus is trying to teach us. Our relation to God depends not accidentally but essentially on the way we respond to those in need. Jesus' revelation of the Eucharist is his response to his own sense of his mission. Luke tells us that at the beginning of his public life, when invited to read from the prophet Isaiah on the Sabbath, "[Jesus] unrolled the scroll and found the place where it was written: 'The spirit of the Lord is upon me, because he has anointed me to bring good news to the poor. He has sent me to proclaim release to the captives and recovery of sight to the blind, to let the oppressed go free, to proclaim the year of the Lord's favor'" (Luke 4:17–19).

How do we link our social concerns and social action with the Eucharist? What prevents us from making the connection that seems so obvious when we think about it and is yet so elusive as an actual motivation, a way of realizing our deepest beliefs and desires? Human weakness and selfishness come into play, but another explanation lies in the way we understand the church.

The justice and peace movement that has developed strongly since the Second Vatican Council emerged at a time when the theology of the church shifted its emphasis from the church as mystical body of Christ to church as the people of God.[3] This shift was necessary in order to correct an overemphasis on the structural, hierarchical dimension of the church. For many people of urban industrialized societies, however, the notion of the church as the people of God is difficult to grasp, because for the most part modern urbanites have not experienced themselves as belonging to a people. The increased job mobility of many persons, with its attendant rootlessness, adds to this difficulty. This does not mean that all the theological riches of the mystery of church as people of God should be neglected, but it does suggest that it might be wise to emphasize as well the metaphor of the church as mystical body of Christ.

The first chapter of the *Dogmatic Constitution on the Church* treats the metaphor of church as mystical body of Christ at some length. It explains that no one symbol or metaphor can adequately express the full reality of the church, and points out four scriptural metaphors that reveal the mystery of the church. These metaphors are from shepherding (John 10:1–10), agriculture (Rom 11:13–26), building construction (1 Cor 3:9), and marriage (Rev 19:7, 21:2).[4] The section on the church as mystical body of Christ follows immediately. It may well be that a stronger connection between Eucharist and social action for justice and peace depends on a fresh recovery of the doctrine of the mystical body of Christ as revealed in scripture and treated in the *Dogmatic Constitution on the Church,* and, at the same time, the integration of this concept with that of church as people of God.

The words of the eucharistic rite offer another rich source for relating Eucharist and social action:

> The day before he suffered, he took bread in his sacred hands and looking up to heaven, to you, his almighty Father, he gave you thanks and praise. He broke the bread, gave it to his disciples, and said, "Take this, all of you, and eat it; this is my body which will be given up for you." When supper was ended, he took the cup. Again he gave you thanks and praise...and said: "Take this, all of you, and drink from it; this is the cup of my blood, the blood of the new and everlasting covenant. It will be shed for you and for all so that sins may be forgiven. Do this in memory of me."[5]

We are to remember that we receive as essential food for our lives, as the strength for our own faith journey, the body of Christ given for us all the way to the acceptance of death, and that Jesus' death was the consequence of his own hunger for justice and his peacemaking rooted in love. We believe in a new covenant in his blood, that is, in the Eucharist as a solemn agreement, a ratification of our own deepest desire to live as he lived in his community of disciples.

The *Catechism* says that the Eucharist is called the Lord's Supper not only because of its connection with the supper on the eve of Jesus' passion and death, but also because it looks forward to the fulfillment of the passion, death, and resurrection of Jesus symbolized by the wedding feast of the Lamb (Rev 19:9). What was characteristic of the early church was joy and energy in sharing in the resurrection of Jesus. Out of the joy of communion, the early Christians both began the transformation of their immediate society and recognized the missionary dimension of their faith. They experienced themselves as both called and sent.

There is a paradox in the life of Jesus that is key to understanding the Eucharist and its import for us: Jesus put an end to death itself not by overcoming it but by undergoing it. He recognized the fundamental truth that unless the grain of wheat dies, it remains just a grain of wheat, but if it dies, it brings forth much fruit. In undergoing death, Jesus was not simply coming to the end of his temporal bodily existence; he was showing the depth of his love, and that is what put an end to death forever. Our lives are to be a participation in Jesus' life and death. We eat the bread of life and drink the saving cup in the new and everlasting covenant. How can we find simple ways to experience this great truth and grow in our appreciation of this mystery?

Saint Paul was upset with the Corinthians because they allowed economic distinctions to wreck the communion of the faithful. Although in our churches we do not celebrate the Sunday Eucharist in the context of an ordinary meal in which some eat well and some eat poorly or not at all, we do live linked together in a world where the distinction is not only in the amount and quality of food but in actual hunger and malnutrition that leads to death. We carry this burden with us all day and all night.

Jesus instituted the Eucharist at a meal with his disciples, and the liturgical reforms of the Second Vatican Council have restored a strong emphasis on the meal aspect of the Eucharist. We may discover that in working out these implications of the Eucharist as the Lord's Supper we will find ways in which our actions for justice and peace are expressions of Christ's kind of love. It may be that it is in actual meals related to the Eucharist that we will discover some creative ways to live a social spirituality.

I once was invited to a parish to give a series of talks during Lent. One talk took place during a "soup supper," an event typical of the kind held weekly in many parishes during Lent. In this particular parish, the soup supper was managed by a committee that recruited four or five parish members each week to supply a pot of soup each for the supper. The soup, with crackers and a beverage, constituted the meal. It was not a pot luck in which a variety of favorite dishes graced the table; rather, the intention was to give the difference in cost between the soup supper and a more expensive meal to a collection divided between national and local Catholic organizations that served poor people through direct action or through advocacy.

I arrived early to chat with parishioners before I gave my presentation. People were just beginning to arrive, and I introduced myself to a couple seated alone. They were retired, and in the course of our conversation the husband told me how good it was to have supper with their friends at church one night a week. His wife said that she enjoyed not having to make supper once a week; in fact, she was sorry to see the soup suppers discontinued at the end of Lent. "Why not keep the soup suppers up as a regular parish activity?" I asked. They told me that they would have to get a speaker, and that would mean a lot of work for someone. I suggested that since the main benefits were unrelated to the speaker, they might think about having soup suppers for the simple joy of getting to know each other better as well as sharing with poor people of the larger community, their city, the nation, and even the world. We talked throughout the simple meal, and meanwhile, teenagers were supervising the play of younger children who finished their meal early; others were doing the cleaning up.

It would take only some modest leadership to make such a supper a widespread weekly practice in parishes. The possibilities are endless. Accompanying the inauguration of a weekly parish meal there could be an explanation linking the meal directly to the Sunday Eucharist as an extension of it. In many parishes we have become accustomed to the beautiful rite that accompanies sending eucharistic ministers to the sick and other homebound in our parishes. There are many kinds of sicknesses in our world, and we are all called to be eucharistic ministers in one way or another. The custom of parish soup suppers has great possibilities for development.

Retreat and Return

The gospel accounts portray Jesus as a man who had a need not only for a community of disciples but also a need to be alone. The two characteristics are related. What did Jesus do when he went off into the hills? We are told that he spent the night in prayer, especially before such particularly crucial moments of his public ministry as the call of the disciples, and his arrest and subsequent passion and death. But we can assume that retreat was a regular feature of his life. Jesus needed solitude as all human beings need it. In order to live a life of depth, we all need time and space to plumb our depths. It is there that we find that we are both alone and not alone, that we are held in existence by the mystery we name God, in whom we live and move and have our being. We experience that we are held in existence by the love of God.

Love is the ground of our lives. It is this power that we want to express in our actions. If we never withdraw from our ordinary activities, our lives can become simply a series of unreflective responses to whatever stimuli happen to predominate at the moment. Good habits—our virtues—keep us from absolute selfishness; but to grow in love requires taking time to be in love. That is what times of prayer are meant to be.

John Main, an English Benedictine and internationally known teacher of a way of centering prayer, wrote of prayer as a way of mature responsibility:

> Our society trains us to remain childish, dependent on external stimuli and amusement, spoon-fed on the prepackaged experiences we call entertainment that have as much spiritual nutrition as the convenience foods that, like television, symbolize our culture. In discovering the existence of such a responsibility in our lives we are tempted and trained to evade it, to retreat yet again into childish distraction and dissipation. The responsibility of making a mature response seems to us like a curtailment of our freedom.

This is why meditation is so important for us all. It prepares us for the real freedom that lives and rejoices at the heart of this mystery of love within us, the movement of divine energy that is also the stillness of our pilgrimage of faith. To pray in the infinite depths of our spirit, which is the depth of God, is to be utterly free.

And our daily meditation, the deepening experience that flowers on the trellis of our discipline, teaches us the essential lesson of maturity: freedom does not consist in doing what we want but in being who we are. To be free is to have been liberated into being by a power of love greater than our own power of ego. It is to have encountered and responded to the Other in humility. The liberty is the liberty to be open to God as the ground of our being—the structure of all reality, inner and outer. It is to be redeemed by love from the slavery of self-consciousness and self-preoccupation.[7]

Each of us has to work out the rhythm of personal prayer according to our responsibilities and situation at different times of our lives. If we do not devote regular space and time to personal contemplation, actions for justice and peace will be like fruits that wither on the vine for want of nourishment. Jesus used this very metaphor:

I am the true vine, and my Father is the vinegrower. He removes every branch in me that bears no fruit. Every branch that bears fruit he prunes to make it bear more fruit. You have already been cleansed by the word that I have spoken to you. Abide in me as I abide in you. Just as the branch cannot bear fruit by itself unless it abides in the vine, neither can you unless you abide in me. I am the vine, you are the branches. Those who abide in me and I in them bear much fruit, because apart from me you can do nothing. (John 15:1–5)

In our culture of continual motion and sound, with homes that rarely may not have a television or radio playing, we need to be ingenious in finding "little Sabbaths," pools of space and time for genuine prayer that requires more than a few hurried moments. Every period in Christian history has seen the emergence of new ways to respond to a given culture's particular needs. Catholic social teaching talks about the "evangelization of culture."[8] We evangelize culture when we bring the values of the gospel to bear on society's beliefs and practices. While beliefs and practices may be less structured than established economic and political institutions, they are equally important as the building blocks of institutions.

Unconventional Retreats

Perhaps we need a new popular movement that can provide unconventional retreats based in parishes. How many parishes have houses that once were homes for large families and are now kept up with difficulty by an elderly couple or a single person? Is it possible that the ministry of hospitality in a parish might include rooms available for a person who needs some quiet time away for a day? Someone who would feel awkward about acknowledging such a need or accepting such a gift of hospitality might be put at ease if such a ministry of hospitality were made a normal part of parish life.

Not everything that is possible is actual, but what is actual is possible. This came home to me when I stayed with a family I was meeting for the first time while on a trip for Pax Christi. There were five children in the family. The parents had recently purchased a large old house that needed a good bit of repair work, and in preparing the house for their family they had been able to finish two bedrooms in what had been the attic. They went to their pastor and told him that they had two spare rooms (I stayed in one on my visit) and that if ever he knew someone who needed a place to stay, he should let them know. The fact that the father of this family is a social worker may have had something to do with this gesture, but it took the entire family to carry out the idea. And carry it out they did. The parents delighted in telling me of a teenager estranged from her family who had spent several months with them and returned home after being reconciled with her parents. There had been several other similar experiences with the two guest rooms, and the overall reaction of the family was how blessed they had been in their guests. I was reminded of Saint John Chrysostom, who said in a sermon:

> Make yourself a guest-chamber in your own house; set up
> a bed there, set up a table there and a candlestick....Have
> a room to which Christ may come. Say, "This is Christ's
> cell; this building is set apart for him." Even though it is
> just a little insignificant room in the basement, he does not
> disdain it. Naked and a stranger, Christ goes about—all he
> wants is shelter. Make it available even though it is as little
> as this.[9]

Restored by retreat, we can return to those with whom we live
and work with a livelier love and energy. We might be inspired to
consider offering a day of respite to someone in our parish who is
caregiver for a loved one suffering from Alzheimer's or any other
debilitating disease. A free day for a caregiver may mean the difference between that person's ability to continue with grace and
their feeling that the task is beyond their capacity. Today there are
groups that organize such respite care and train those who want
to offer this kind of service. What a beautiful extension of
Eucharist respite care can be.

An Order of Saving Beauty

Times of retreat are times for contemplation. To contemplate
is to pay attention. Just as service can bring us into contact with
God under the aspect of goodness in others, and as social analysis
and advocacy about issues of justice and peace can bring us into
contact with God under the aspect of truth, contemplation can
bring us into touch with God under the aspect of beauty. Dorothy
Day was fond of quoting Dostoevsky's saying that beauty would
save the world. Perhaps the time is ripe for founding an Order of
Saving Beauty, which might begin by trying to bring beauty into
places that badly need it.

A police station is one such place. I became acutely aware of
this when I spent some time in a police station as chief witness of
an assault in which a person standing next to me had been shot
and my coat bore the bloody evidence of the gunshot wound. I
had to return to the scene with a detective and then go to the
police station to describe in great detail what had happened. At
the end of the interrogation, I was told that if I waited for a half-
hour one of the officers would drive me home. As I sat there in a

semi-traumatized state that I did not even recognize, I was sharply aware of the griminess of the place where I was sitting: the floor that needed scrubbing and waxing, the drab furniture, and especially the lack of anything tasteful, let alone beautiful. That was the beginning of an idea of how good it would be if high school and college art students could be encouraged and even organized a bit to hang some of their work in local police stations, with the understanding that they would return within a few months and present the station with something new. The same offer could be made any number of other places.

An Order of Seasonal Hermits

Perhaps in our time there is also need for an Order of Seasonal Hermits. I once said this half in jest at a time when I myself experienced a call to a solitary time for more than a few days, and managed to find a hermitage where I was able to stay for a month. A few years later I repeated the experience. In conversing about it with friends, and especially when I broached the idea of an Order of Seasonal Hermits, I was amazed at the positive response. At one point someone actually tracked me down and wanted more information about this "Order" with the intention of possibly joining it! Meanwhile, I had discovered not a few places where the need, place, and time for being a short-term hermit had come together.

For one dear friend the place was her automobile. Recognizing the need for a time of solitude after the death of her husband, she drove alone from coast to coast over a period of three weeks, traveling at her own pace and taking generous time for rest and prayer. She visited a few friends she had not been able to see during her husband's long illness, and she revisited places rich in memories of times spent with her husband. She returned refreshed in soul and body from her mobile retreat.

"The fullness of joy is to behold God in everything," wrote Julian of Norwich.[10] Creative practices of hospitality, the Order of Saving Beauty, and the Order of Seasonal Hermits are a few of a myriad of possible ways to participate in the universal call to act for justice and peace as a community of disciples of Jesus, ways that create and nourish the context in which efforts for economic and political change become more possible.

QUESTIONS FOR STUDY, REFLECTION, AND CONVERSATION

1. How do you make connections between Eucharist and hungry people?
2. What do you understand by the "new and everlasting covenant" inaugurated by Jesus?
3. If Saint Paul were to comment on a celebration of the Eucharist in your parish, what might he say?
4. What would it take to have a simple supper as an extension of the Eucharist on a regular basis in your parish? How would you explain the purpose of the meal to a visitor?
5. Are you able to find "little Sabbaths"? Why are they important?
6. What do the words of Saint John Chrysostom on page 26 suggest to you?
7. Find out if respite care is formally organized in your parish.
8. Imagine yourself as a member of the Order of Saving Beauty or the Order of Seasonal Hermits, or of some other group you have founded. Describe your way of life and ministry.

NOTES

1. *Catechism of the Catholic Church*, Libreria Editrice Vaticana. English trans. U.S. Catholic Conference (Liguori, MO: Liguori, 1994), II, 1328–32.

2. John R. Donahue, SJ, "Do You Really Believe That?" *America*, June 4–11, 2001, 31.

3. John A. Coleman, SJ, "How the Eucharist Proclaims Social Justice: Part Two," *Church*, Spring 2001, 12. Coleman refers to Keith Pecklers, SJ, *The Unread Vision: The Liturgical Movement in the United States of America 1926–1955* (Collegeville, MN: Liturgical Press, 1998). Coleman writes, "Pecklers laments, at the end of his study, the displacement of the rich social notion of the Mystical Body of Christ by Vatican II's more individualistic concept of a diverse 'people of God.'"

4. *Dogmatic Constitution on the Church (Lumen Gentium)*, art. 6, in Walter A. Abbott, SJ, *The Documents of Vatican II* (New York: Herder

and Herder, 1966), 18–20. All subsequent references to documents of the Second Vatican Council are from this edition.

5. Roman Missal, Eucharistic Prayer I.

6. *Catechism of the Catholic Church*, II, 1329.

7. Paul Harris, ed., *Silence and Stillness in Every Season: Daily Readings with John Main* (New York: Continuum, 1998), 284.

8. *Gaudium et Spes*, arts. 53–62, pp. 201–8; *Evangelii Nuntiandi*, art. 20, p. 310; *Centesimus Annus*, arts. 51–52, pp. 477–79, in David J. O'Brien and Thomas A. Shannon, eds., in *Catholic Social Thought: The Documentary Heritage* (Maryknoll, NY: Orbis, 1992).

9. William J. Walsh and John P. Langan, "Patristic Social Consciousness—The Church and the Poor," in John C. Haughey, ed., *The Faith That Does Justice: Examining the Christian Sources for Social Change* (New York: Paulist Press, 1977), 132.

10. Julian of Norwich, *Showings* (New York: Paulist Press, 1978), 190.

CHAPTER THREE

— ✣ —

The Healing Power of Nonviolence

The message about the cross is foolishness to those who are
perishing, but to us who are being saved it is the power of
God....For God's foolishness is wiser than human wisdom,
and God's weakness is stronger than human strength.
—1 Corinthians 1:18, 25

No longer do we take the sword against any nation nor do
we learn war any more since we have become the sons of
peace through Jesus.
—Origen (d. 254)

CHAPTER FOCUS

The goal of active nonviolence is reconciliation. It is crucially important to human and social development. Violence is often an expression of a deep, unhealed wound. Active nonviolence, which seeks to heal rather than to injure or destroy, requires a commitment to restorative justice and a decision to forgive—that is, a decision not to let a past injury determine present and future attitudes and actions. Two basic skills of active nonviolence are compassionate listening and looking at others with benevolence. Catholic social teaching on nonviolence in the context of war is developing, as is demonstrated by comparing the U.S. bishops' 1983 pastoral letter on peace with their statement on the tenth anniversary of that letter.

A Process of Reconciling

To understand active nonviolence, we begin by looking at reconciliation as the goal of nonviolence. Whether people see nonviolence as a strategy or understand it as a way of life, nonviolence is motivated by a desire for reconciliation. Acts of violence, war, and the bitter memories they leave behind drive people apart and keep them apart unless they achieve reconciliation. Unhealed wounds that fester underground need only the provocation of fresh hurts to set off another phase in a spiral of violence. This has always been the human condition, both on the interpersonal level and in the public arena. The spiral of violence is a bloody hemorrhage in the human race.

Peace movements by the hundreds come and go with the particular issues that they address. Among these movements, a few last well beyond particular wars or other crises. The International Fellowship of Reconciliation, founded in 1914, and Pax Christi International, which began in 1945, are two such movements that are stronger today than when they began. Each was founded during a world war by persons of religious faith, and in both cases their members had their eyes less on the war than on the prize: the desire for reconciliation between warring peoples who needed healing of terrible wounds, not all of them physical. The process of healing throws light on what is called for in reconciliation.

Healing

My earliest recollection of healing is of being kissed by my mother when I had hurt myself. Mothers instinctively know what to do: they heal with an expression of love and caring. Not all wounds are so quickly healed as the scraped knees of a small child, but love is undoubtedly the most potent healer and, in a very true sense, the only one. Not all hurts are physical. We can get a clearer and richer idea of reconciliation if we approach it as a process of healing wounded relationships.

Reconciliation, the healing of wounded or broken relationships, is a gift of openness to God's motherlike healing love. It is in the heart that relationships are made and nourished, and also sometimes wounded and broken. Reconciliation requires the healing of deep wounds in a relationship. We are made for friendship, and a friendly climate is the only one in which human development, personal or social, ordinarily can take place. The very word *enemy* comes from a Latin word, *inimicus,* which means "not a friend." Whereas enemies express their relationship in hurtful ways, ways of violence, friends express their relationship in caring, supportive ways. Reconciliation restores harmony and a friendly relationship between two or more persons or groups that have been at odds with each other.

Reconciliation is crucially important because we realize our full humanity only in good relationships. There is always a blockage in the development of the person who acts violently. Psychologists tell us that the source of every act of violence is an unhealed wound. If the person who is the object of violence responds in kind, the blockage or wound in the violator is made worse. To restore the flow of love that is the very life of good relationships, the wound must be acknowledged so that the cycle of violence can be altered. This requires an inner stillness and peace that enables one to be attentive to the other. Even without speaking, a person can communicate respectful attention, care, and the desire to understand the other's perception of a situation that is standing in the way of reconciliation. This is an ongoing process, not one event or a single accomplishment. Perhaps we do well to use the words *reconciling* or *reconciling process* in an effort to come to a clearer and richer idea of what reconciliation is all about.

Forgiveness and Restorative Justice

There can be no reconciliation without a concern for justice. This requires a courageous facing of facts, however painful they may be. But facts can be faced with scorn and a sense of self-righteousness and superiority, or with compassion. If we know ourselves and our society well, we will be aware that there is need for repentance and sincere expression of sorrow and forgiveness on all sides. Forgiveness is not primarily a feeling but a decision, a decision not to let the wrongs one has suffered be the determining factor in a relationship that is in need of repair. Just as forgiveness is a decision, so the refusal to forgive is also a decision, one that locks an unforgiving person into a prison of bitterness and loneliness. Forgiveness is not easy, but its fruit is great freedom and peace, even though feelings of hurt and even spontaneous desires for revenge are likely to persist. A person is in a better position to deal with these feelings and to move forward constructively once he or she has made the decision to forgive.

Reconciliation aims for restorative justice, which emphasizes the relationship that is sought for and is more concerned about the persons involved than about the issues on the table, though the issues must be faced. Justice may require reparation and restitution on the part of the offender; however, if this requirement is imposed in a spirit of vengeance, it will provoke vengeance in turn. The overarching goal of restorative justice is to bring the offender back into participation in the community. It is the very opposite of retaliation or retribution in a spirit of vindictiveness. Gandhi shrewdly observed that an eye for an eye and a tooth for a tooth would leave the whole world blind and toothless. The decision to forgive includes more than letting go of a hurt; it includes a fundamental posture of care for the other. The desire to get even and to pay back is a reflex that is counter to the way of Jesus, whose teaching is clear and straightforward. "But I say to you that listen, Love your enemies, do good to those who hate you, bless those who curse you, pray for those who abuse you" (Luke 6:27–28).

The gratitude that accompanies sincere efforts at reconciliation needs to find expression in some visible way that nurtures the ongoing reconciling process. This can be as simple as a handshake or as lavish as throwing a grand party after the manner of the prodigal son's father (Luke 15:21–24). In many cultures, to have a meal together is a way to celebrate reconciliation. As people share food that is a gift from God, they can more easily experience the truth that reconciliation itself is a gift of God's own peace.

Reconciliation with God is the necessary foundation of lasting reconciliation between people. Unfortunately, we may have been brought up on a seriously faulty theology that presented Jesus' death as payment of a debt to God in a way that portrays God the father as someone who needed to even a score. This is hardly different from vengeance, and is clearly not the meaning of Jesus' death. Rather, Jesus' death is a revelation of the extent of his love, which is the extent of God's own love. "For the love of Christ urges us on, because we are convinced that one has died for all; therefore all have died. And he died for all, so that those who live might live no longer for themselves, but for him who died and was raised for them" (2 Cor 5:14–15). This is the revelation of a love that is stronger than death, the love of Jesus risen from the dead, the love that makes all things new. When we experience reconciliation, we find ourselves in a grateful, loving relationship with God who heals us with the gift of peace and sends us out to continue his own work of reconciliation. Our way is active nonviolence, which calls us to develop all our human powers.

Using Our Senses

Compassionate listening is a fundamental practice of active nonviolence. It is not a vague intention to be sensitive to another's hurt; rather, it requires empathy, understanding, and the careful cultivation of specific skills. Gene Knudsen-Hoffman, who has devoted much of her life to developing and teaching this deeply human art, explains that compassionate listening is largely about developing constructive attitudes toward the other with whom there is a disagreement or conflict. She often speaks of the suffering of those in a conflict. In an interview she told me:

> My experience over the years convinces me that in every serious situation there is deep suffering on both sides; both sides are wounded. *Compassion* means "to suffer with." The point of compassionate listening is to enable that suffering to find expression in a healing context.
>
> Conflict is about much more than solving a problem. Dealing well with conflict often involves healing of deep hurts on both sides. It is a mistake to think first in terms of who is right and who is wrong; first, we need to listen sensitively to the pain carried by all parties in a conflict. We have to listen for the grievances, how people hurt; we have to open ourselves to listen to their anger. Some terrorists, for example, think that they will never get a hearing, that their grievances will not be addressed, so they turn to violence.

This explains why the most basic step is training in attitude. Here, practice in reflection on one's own behavior is important. Gene has her students ask themselves if they see "something of the divine" in every person. Can they listen with a "spiritual ear" for that depth dimension in the other person and also in themselves? Can they hear some truth on both sides of a dispute or conflict? Do they respect the right of persons to differ as they are trying to work through conflict?

Built on these attitudes there are three basic steps in the practice of compassionate listening. First, each side tells the other of their own pain and grievances in the situation. Second, each side tells the other how they understand the other's explanation of their own pains and grievances. They stay with this step until each side agrees that both sides have adequately described the other side's pain. In a serious dispute, the two sides may first agree on a facilitator to guide this process. These first two steps prepare the context for resolving a conflict. It is a process in which each side tries to enter into the feelings of the other side before they move into a discussion of the perceived issues of the conflict. Third, if appropriate, they move to a win-win negotiation process. At this point a facilitator or mediator can often be very helpful.

At the request of Vietnamese Buddhist monk, peacemaker, and poet Thich Nhat Hanh, who has been one of her teachers, Gene organized a retreat for a group of U.S. veterans of the war in Vietnam. The hope was that the veterans, who had severe psychological wounds from their participation in the war, could come back to society as healed and creative people. During the retreat, the participants talked about violence in which they had been personally involved. Before he came to the retreat, one veteran, who had killed twelve children in a village, had hardly left his room since his return to the United States. Considerable healing took place among the veterans who were present. Some of them returned to Vietnam, where they helped with construction work in a village.

Adam Curle, founder emeritus of the peace studies program at Bradford University in England, is another well-known practitioner of compassionate listening. He served as mediator in Nigeria and Sri Lanka during wars in these countries. A longtime Quaker, his beginning point in listening is a belief in a divine element in each person that is ever available to help in bringing about harmony. His posture toward others is one of befriending. He explains what happens when a person listens with care:

Listening does not only lead to hearing and understanding, but also to speech. If we learn to listen, we will often find that the right words are given to us. These do not come as a result of careful thought, but spring from our more profound sources of knowledge. The importance of listening, then, is not only that we "hear" the other in a profound sense but communicate with him or her through our true nature. For this reason very strong and positive feelings are often aroused in both the listener and the one listened to. In this way peacemakers may reach the part of the other person that is really able to make peace, outwardly as well as inwardly.[1]

Akin to compassionate listening is benevolent glancing. In Western culture, we are conditioned to think of our eyes as tools for extracting data. We take a picture, for example, or take a look at something. Somewhere along the way, I learned that Buddhists use their eyes for receiving rather than taking. They see reality as moving toward them, and this requires that they position themselves to receive it. It is a posture of appreciative receiving rather than taking, an experience I call "benevolent glancing."

My experiments with benevolent glancing began when I cut from the newspaper a small item about Pope John Paul II's visit with the Supreme Patriarch of the Buddhists of Thailand during John Paul's visit to Southeast Asia during the 1980s. Protocol for the visit required that the two men sit together for some time in absolute silence while they exchanged "fraternal glances." (Inadvertently I had changed "fraternal" to "benevolent" when I started to repeat the story, as I discovered much later when I located again the original clipping.) I wondered what it felt like to exchange benevolent glances with a stranger. What was the difference between just plain looking and benevolent glancing? The question so intrigued me that I decided to look for an opportunity to experiment.

I have spent a fair amount of my life on public transportation. Not long after I read the story about the pope and the patriarch, I found an opportunity to give benevolent glancing a try while I was on a long bus ride in Chicago. Because I did not try to find a partner, it was a one-way experiment. A strange thing happened. I found that I was praying—not saying prayers, but being attentive, alert, and aware in a way difficult to describe. For whatever reason, I wanted to look with love on each person who came within my view. Love is what benevolence is all about: the word *benevolence* means "to wish another well."

Since that first experiment, I have learned that to practice benevolent glancing is to experience deeply stirred emotions, ranging from embarrassment and fear to compassion and almost always to love. Fear of invading another person's privacy explains the embarrassment, because there is a fine but clearly distinguishable line between benevolent glancing and staring. We can keep on the right side of the line by modesty, a way of respect, reverence, even awe in the presence of the splendor of the human person, of whom the psalmist wrote, "Yet you have made them a little lower than God, and crowned them with glory and honor" (Ps 8:6).

One time during the height of the nuclear arms race in the 1980s, when I was practicing benevolent glancing on a crowded flight home after a meeting of a peace organization, my attention was drawn to a young mother and her baby boy. How fragile, how absolutely dependent for survival he was, and how marvelous. Looking at the mother and her baby, I kept thinking of her hope for his future and of his promise. I could not escape the fact that God became one of us, just like that baby. I was astounded with the thought of all that hangs on this central mystery of God's love saving us from inside our own flesh and bone, nerve and muscle, mind and heart. If we are to be saved from the consequences of permitting the nuclear arms competition and other injustices that can drive us to destruction, it will be as a gift, the gift to accept ourselves as we truly are: fragile, weak, disordered—yet loved and loving, a little less than the angels, entrusted with each other's lives. How delicate is the balance on which our survival depends!

Appreciation and admiration for other persons evokes an active benevolence, a desire for the true good of the other person. This only rarely translates into an immediate particular act for the person, but it does deeply affect the one who is practicing benevolent glancing. When an occasion arises for a response to a problematic situation, a benevolent glancer may be more apt to act constructively than would a person who has not carefully cultivated the habit of lovingly paying attention.

In prayer we can find ourselves drawn to look benevolently at Jesus in any of the events of his life recorded in the gospel. We learn that there is no need to do a lot of analytic thinking. Just as the worn face of a person on the bus will slowly reveal itself to us if we are simply there attentively, patiently, without demanding, without trying to take anything, so will benevolent glancing at a mystery in the life of Jesus prepare us for surprising gifts of insight and love. Benevolent glancing also works in reverse. Sometimes it is good to rest quietly in the presence of the risen Christ, enjoying his benevolent gaze at us. We may find ourselves drawn into his benevolent gaze at our world, or at a part of it that is of special concern to us at any particular time.

We are called to be attentive to all that is good, all that is wounded, all that is beautiful, all that is marred—learning to see with eyes of love. "Now the Lord is the Spirit, and where the Spirit of the Lord is, there is freedom. And all of us, with unveiled faces, seeing the glory of the Lord as though reflected in a mirror, are being transformed into the same image from one degree of glory to another; for this comes from the Lord, the Spirit" (2 Cor 3:17–18).

Nonviolence in Catholic Social Teaching

Nonviolence is anything but a static concept in Catholic social teaching. With Pope John XXIII and the Second Vatican Council, nonviolence in the form of conscientious objection to military service was recognized as a morally legitimate option for individuals. A more comprehensive understanding of nonviolence has continued to evolve under the pressure of events, especially the horrors of modern warfare and the threat of the nuclear weapons capability of a growing number of states, with the United States of America in the lead in nuclear weapons capability.

When the bishops of the United States wrote their 1983 pastoral letter *The Challenge of Peace: God's Promise and Our Response,* the immediate context was the nuclear arms race based on the very real capability of mutually assured destruction. Those who lobbied earnestly for a consideration of nonviolence in the pastoral letter were heard with respect. Although the letter presents the traditional teaching about the conditions for a just war as normative, it also contains the most developed treatment of nonviolence, based on the gospel accounts of the life and teaching of

Jesus, of any pastoral letter that had ever come from the United States Conference of Catholic Bishops. The letter presents nonviolence as a morally praiseworthy position for individuals. Especially relevant to this teaching is the following passage from the section of the letter on Jesus and the reign of God:

> The words of Jesus would remain an impossible, abstract ideal were it not for two things: the actions of Jesus and his gift of the spirit. In his actions, Jesus showed the way of living in God's reign; he manifested the forgiveness which he called for when he accepted all who came to him, forgave their sins, healed them, released them from the demons who possessed them. In doing these things, he made the tender mercy of God present in a world which knew violence, oppression, and injustice. Jesus pointed out the injustices of his time and opposed those who laid burdens upon the people or defiled true worship. He acted aggressively and dramatically at times, as when he cleansed the temple of those who had made God's house into a "den of robbers" (Matt 21:12–17 and parallel texts; John 3:13–25).
>
> Most characteristic of Jesus' actions are those in which he showed his love. As he had commanded others, his love led him even to the giving of his own life to effect redemption. Jesus' message and his actions were dangerous ones in his time and they led to his death—a cruel and viciously inflicted death, a criminal's death (Gal 3:13). In all of his suffering, as in all of his life and ministry, Jesus refused to defend himself with force or with violence. He endured violence and cruelty so that God's love might be fully manifest and the world might be reconciled to the One from whom it had become estranged. Even at his death, Jesus cried out for forgiveness for those who were his executioners: "Father, forgive them...(Luke 23:34)."[2]

After briefly surveying the Christian teaching and practice of nonviolence from the earliest times to the present, the letter recognizes that "the vision of Christian nonviolence is not passive about injustice and the defense of the rights of others; it rather affirms and exemplifies what it means to resist injustice through nonviolent methods." It goes on to mention Gandhi, Dorothy Day, and Martin Luther King Jr. as exemplars of active nonviolence, and says that the witness of numerous other Christians who had preceded them over the centuries "was affirmed in a remarkable way at the Second Vatican Council." This affirmation includes paragraph 79 of *The Church in the Modern World,* in which the council fathers called upon governments to enact laws protecting the rights of those who adopted the position of conscientious objection to all war.

It is in this section on nonviolence that the bishops also call attention to another very significant passage in *The Church in the Modern World:*

> In the development of a theology of peace and the growth of the Christian pacifist position among Catholics, these words of the Pastoral Constitution have special significance: "All these factors force us to undertake a completely fresh appraisal of war." The Council fathers had reference to "the development of armaments by modern science (which) has immeasurably magnified the horrors and wickedness of war." While the just-war teaching has clearly been in possession for the past 1500 years of Catholic thought, the "new moment" in which we find ourselves sees the just-war teaching and nonviolence as distinct but interdependent methods of evaluating warfare. They diverge on some specific conclusions, but they share a common presumption against the use of force as a means of settling disputes.
>
> Both find their roots in the Christian theological tradition; each contributes to the full moral vision we need in pursuit of a human peace. We believe the two perspectives support and complement one another, each preserving the other from distortion. Finally, in an age of technological warfare, analysis from the viewpoint of nonviolence and analysis from the viewpoint of the just-war teaching often converge and agree in their opposition to methods of warfare which are in fact indistinguishable from total warfare (par. 120–121).[3]

This passage is quoted at length here because it represents a compromise on the part of the bishops who in effect gave strong support to the just-war teaching. In a section on the Presumption against War and the Principle of Legitimate Self-Defense, they wrote:

We believe work to develop nonviolent means of fending off aggression and resolving conflict best reflects the call of Jesus both to love and to justice. Indeed, each increase in the potential destructiveness of weapons and therefore of war serves to underline the rightness of the way that Jesus mandated to his followers. But, on the other hand, the fact of aggression, oppression, and injustice in our world also serves to legitimate the resort to weapons and armed force in defense of justice. We must recognize the reality of the paradox we face as Christians living in the context of the world as it presently exists; we must continue to articulate our belief that love is possible and the only real hope for all human relations, and yet accept that force, even deadly force, is sometimes justified and that nations must provide for their defense. It is the mandate of Christians, in the face of this paradox, to strive to resolve it through an even greater commitment to Christ and his message.[4]

To give added weight to this passage, the bishops conclude with a long excerpt from the 1982 World Day of Peace Message of Pope John Paul II:

Christians are aware that plans based on aggression, domination and the manipulation of others lurk in human hearts, and sometimes even secretly nourish human intentions, in spite of certain declarations or manifestations of a pacifist nature. For Christians know that in this world a totally and peaceful human society is unfortunately a utopia, and that ideologies that hold up that prospect as easily attainable are based on hopes that cannot be realized, whatever the reason behind them. It is a question of a mistaken view of the human condition, a lack of application in considering the question as a whole; or it may be a case of evasion in order to calm fear....This is why Christians, even as they strive to resist and prevent every form of warfare, have no hesitation in recalling that, in the name of an elementary requirement of justice, peoples have a right and even a duty to protect their existence and freedom by proportionate means against an unjust aggressor.[5]

On balance, it must be admitted that while the 1983 pastoral letter gives nonviolence some consideration, it does not accept nonviolence as normative in Catholic social teaching. Killing others in war is taught as a sometimes morally acceptable position. But this was not the last time the bishops of the United States wrote formally about nonviolence.

In 1993 they issued a tenth-anniversary statement on *The Challenge of Peace: God's Promise and Our Response.* The title of their anniversary statement is itself instructive. It is a quotation from the New Testament Letter of James: "The Harvest of Justice Is Sown in Peace." In the first section, "Theology, Spirituality, and Ethics for Peacemaking," they again take up the topic of nonviolence in a section titled "Two Traditions: Nonviolence and the Just War." The fact that nonviolence is given first place in their treatment is significant. They wrote:

> The Christian tradition possesses two ways to address conflict: nonviolence and just war. They both share the common goal: to diminish violence in this world....It is the how of defending peace which offers moral options. We take up this dual tradition again recognizing, on the one hand, the success of nonviolent methods in recent history and, on the other, the increasing disorder of the post–Cold War world with its pressures for limited military engagement and humanitarian intervention.
>
> Throughout history there has been a shifting relation between the two streams of the tradition which always remain in tension. Like Christians before us who have sought to read the signs of the times in light of this dual tradition, we today struggle to assess the lessons of the nonviolent revolutions in Eastern Europe in 1989 and the former Soviet Union in 1991, on the one hand, and of the conflicts in Central America, the Persian Gulf, Bosnia, Somalia, Lebanon, Cambodia and Northern Ireland on the other.[6]

The bishops point out that "the high level of civilian deaths raises serious moral questions about political choices and military doctrines which have had such tragic results over the last half century. The presumption against the use of force has also been strengthened by the examples of the nonviolence in some places in Eastern Europe and elsewhere." After reviewing their earlier position they say:

> Ten years after our pastoral letter, recent events raise new questions and concerns which need to be addressed:
>
> *Nonviolence: new importance.* As *The Challenge of Peace* observed, "the vision of Christian nonviolence is not passive about injustice and the defense of the rights of others." It ought not be confused with popular notions of nonresisting pacifism. For it consists of a commitment to resist manifest injustice and public evil with means other than force. These include dialogue, negotiations, protests, strikes, boycotts, civil disobedience and civilian resistance. Although nonviolence has often been regarded as simply a personal option or vocation, *recent history suggests that in some circumstances it can be an effective public undertaking as well. Dramatic political transitions in places as diverse as the Philippines and Eastern Europe demonstrate the power of nonviolent action even against dictatorial and totalitarian regimes.* (Emphasis mine)[7]

Again the bishops quote Pope John Paul II to reinforce their position:

> Writing about the events of 1989, Pope John Paul II said: "It seemed that the European order resulting from the Second World War...could only be overturned by another war. Instead, it has been overcome by the nonviolent commitment of people who, while always refusing to yield to the force of power, succeeded time after time in finding effective ways of bearing witness to the truth."
>
> These nonviolent revolutions challenge us to find ways to take into full account the power of organized, active nonviolence. What is the real potential power of serious nonviolent strategies and tactics—and their limits? What are the ethical requirements when organized nonviolence fails to overcome evil and when totalitarian powers inflict massive injustice on an entire people? What are the responsibilities of and limits on the international community?

One must ask, in light of recent history, whether nonviolence should be restricted to personal commitments or whether it also should have a place in the public order with the tradition of justified and limited war. National leaders bear a moral obligation to see that non–violent alternatives are seriously considered for dealing with conflicts. New styles of preventative diplomacy and conflict resolution ought to be explored, tried, improved and supported. As a nation we should promote research, education and training in nonviolent means of resisting evil. Nonviolent strategies need greater attention in international affairs. [Emphasis mine]

Such obligations do not detract from a state's right and duty to defend against aggression as a last resort. They do, however, raise the threshold for the recourse to force by establishing institutions which promote nonviolent solutions of disputes and nurturing political commitment to such efforts. In some future conflicts, strikes and people power could be more effective than guns and bullets.[8]

Clearly, nonviolence has moved closer to the center of Catholic social teaching on peace and war. Since the passage just quoted was written, the world is experiencing a new kind of international conflict in which terrorism has forced another change in the way we think about war and ways of defense. This may be a moment in which nonviolence is given more attention than ever before and its consistency with the gospel is made clearer to the church.

QUESTIONS FOR STUDY, REFLECTION, AND CONVERSATION

1. Reconciliation is the goal of active nonviolence. How does this goal differ from the goal of war? Of other kinds of violence?
2. What is restorative justice? What is its function in relation to capital punishment? To war?
3. What is the difference between forgiveness as a decision and forgiveness as an emotion? Can you recall an experience of each? In the light of this distinction, what does it mean to love our enemies? What are the practical consequences?
4. What is the difference between restitution and retribution?

5 Compassionate listening and benevolent seeing are personal practices. What are their significance for social conflicts? For international relations?

6. Given the development of the U.S. bishops' teaching on nonviolence, what do you foresee as further developments? On what will these developments depend?

NOTES

1. Adam Curle, *Tools for Transformation: A Personal Study* (Stroud, UK: Hawthorne Press, 1990), 50–51.

2. *The Challenge of Peace,* arts. 48–49, p. 502, in David J. O'Brien and Thomas A. Shannon, eds., *Catholic Social Thought: The Documentary Heritage* (Maryknoll, NY: Orbis, 1992).

3. Ibid., arts. 116–21, p. 518.

4. Ibid., art. 78, p. 510.

5. Ibid.

6. U.S. Bishops, "The Harvest of Justice Is Sown in Peace," *Origins* 23 (26), December 9, 1993: 453–54.

7. Ibid.

8. Ibid.

CHAPTER FOUR

— ❖ —

How Nonviolence Works

If we could read the secret history of our enemies, we should find in each person's life sorrow and suffering enough to disarm all hostility.
—Henry Wadsworth Longfellow

Of power there are two kinds: one is obtained through threats of punishment, the other arises from acts of love.
—Mohandas Gandhi

CHAPTER FOCUS

Violence is power used to injure and kill; it may be in the form of physical or military force or in the form of unjust political and economic structures. Active nonviolence is power used to heal, to reconcile, and to nurture life and growth. There is an urgent need for nonviolent alternatives to war and to the violence of political-economic injustice in today's highly interdependent world. Hospitality is proposed as a root metaphor that can help one grasp the possibilities of active nonviolence. Active nonviolence, which is a way of dealing with conflicts at all levels, requires attitudes, understandings, and skills that can be learned.

Understanding Violence

Nonviolence is not the absence of violence, but its opposite. Both are modes of power. Violence is force used to injure. We instinctively shrink from it because it leads in the direction of death. We do not understand human death by violence as a natu-

46

ral death. Although some animals kill human beings violently, we intuitively recognize that killing by an animal is not so terrible as the deliberate killing, by one human being, of another human being or of many others. We know that while human beings sometimes kill accidentally, they also kill with some measure of deliberation and responsibility, and it is this killing that is unnerving.

Killing not only evokes revulsion; it also fascinates, and one reason is that it expresses enormous power over life. The beginning of a human life is found in a free act of God who loves each creature into existence through the ways of nature, including cases where there is considerable use of technological intervention in the process. While we can cooperate in creating human life, but no more than that, we can destroy life, and that is heady power. Anyone who doubts this has only to watch television in the United States for a week. Unless we recognize that there is pleasure in fantasies of power associated with violence, and particularly the violence of killing, we may never be able to understand the complexity of the institutionalized killing we know as war. Our cultural myth is that killing in war, at least in the wars in which our country is involved, occurs only for a noble purpose and under conditions of extreme heroism. This is a partial story, and not completely accurate. In the heat of battle, men experience not only great fear but, in the case of some, also a feeling of extraordinary power bordering on the illusion of omnipotence.[1]

There is uneasiness about killing in war, reflected in the way we talk about it. Conventional language uses such expressions as "casualties" rather than victims, and "use of force" rather than killing, in order to mask the reality of violent killing. In the killing of civilians there is even greater uneasiness, stemming from a long moral tradition that war is tolerable only between combatants. Civilians who are killed are described as "collateral damage." Policymakers in nations where there is a Christian heritage will point out that killing civilians is never directly intended, while acknowledging that the approved military operations will kill civilians. This kind of reasoning would not be tolerated in a court in the case of killing outside of war.

Modern technology wed to the acceptance of killing in war has given the world not only genocidal weapons, but weapons that can rightly be called "omnicidal," that is, weapons that can end civilization as we know it and as it has developed over the course of millennia. The fact that these high-tech weapons of mass destruction are out of reach for most countries is a factor in the growing preoccupation with chemical and biological weapons. Chemical and biological weapons, as well as other acts of terrorism that do not come within conventionally accepted rules of war, are perceived as alternatives by some who feel that they must use violence in the pursuit of their own goals but do not have access to the kind of weaponry made by the United States and some other highly industrialized countries. This should help us see the importance of coming to grips with nonviolence in the search for alternatives to war.

The Power of Nonviolence

Nonviolence is not the absence of violence, but its opposite. Nonviolence not only refuses to use killing power or acts that lead to it, but also offers an alternative. Nonviolence is power to heal, to reconcile, to resolve conflicts, to nurture life and growth. All these characteristics and more apply both to nonviolence in interpersonal human relations and to relations on the societal level, including conflicts that lead to war.

Although we do not find the term *nonviolence* in the gospel, it is clear that nonviolence is not only consistent with the life and teaching of Jesus but is at the very heart of his life and teaching. Nonviolence is not passivity but a strong force springing from a worldview that sees the parties to a conflict as fundamentally good, coupled with a deep trust in the power of goodness to bring about change for the better. It is very unfortunate that the negative term *nonviolence* serves to describe something so positive. Gandhi, the great experimenter with nonviolence on the societal level in South Africa early in his career and later in India, was sensitive to the disadvantages of the term *nonviolence,* which is too easily equated with passivity or with a reluctance to show the courage needed in cases where defense is a moral obligation. In a newspaper Gandhi edited in South Africa, he ran a contest to coin a term to describe his method of dealing with oppression. Thus he came up with the term *satyagraha,* a compound of two Sanskrit words, *sat,* meaning "reality" or "truth," and *agraha,* meaning "to grasp firmly." *Satyagraha,* which today is frequently translated as *nonviolence,* means "to hold on firmly to the truth."

What, specifically, is this truth? For Gandhi, truth meant God. Gandhi saw truth as always emerging in a conflict when one side, at least, refused to harm an opponent even if the opponent did not reciprocate in kind. According to Gandhi, the practitioner of *satyagraha* must be determined not to inflict violence, while at the same time be willing to suffer violence if that is necessary to witness to truth in a given situation. *Satyagraha* is not passivity, but an alternative way of defense requiring great courage, discipline, and specific skills. It is moral power brought into play especially in situations where conflict is about to erupt into violence or has already done so. The violence in question may be in the form of economic and social injustice as well as armed violence.

Gandhi said that there are two kinds of power: one obtained by threats of punishment, the other arising from acts of love. Nonviolence is the second kind of power. We are all familiar with it, and practice it regularly in our ongoing relationships, whether with spouses, children, clients, colleagues, or neighbors and friends. We are not always explicitly conscious of this power as arising from acts of love, but when we stop to think about it there is no other source of good deeds we do from a desire for the well-being of others. Goodness far outweighs evil in our world, or we would not be here to continue the history of goodness. What we are looking at is the possibility of enlarging the field of the goodness, of active nonviolence in situations of conflict, small and large.[2]

Nonviolence and Hospitality

Abide in me as I abide in you.
—John 15:4

It is in the shelter of each other that the people live.
—Gaelic saying

The particular quality of love that is prominent in nonviolence is *caring*. Milton Mayeroff has written an insightful book, *On Caring,* in which he develops the thesis that a person is at home in the world not by dominating, not even by understanding or appreciating, but by caring and being cared for.[3] The word *care* here includes the notion of deep concern for another, an attention marked by affection. It comes from an old Germanic word meaning "to cry out." Care implies emotional involvement and compassion, a capacity to enter into another's suffering, a willingness to share the situation of another and to spend oneself for another. Significantly, Mayeroff related caring to being "at home in the world." Though there are many different kinds of dwelling places, we all know that a house of itself does not make a home. To be at home refers to a particular kind of relationship. When we say that we feel at home with someone, we mean that we are at ease, that we feel mutual trust and concern, that we experience an inner freedom that enables us to relax and share what is on our mind and heart. Sometimes we feel more at home with a person who knows less about us than with others who have known us for a long time. In caring, the dominant note is not understanding, but concern.

There is an important clue about nonviolence in the connection between home and caring that leads us to consider the possibility of an overarching metaphor for nonviolence. The metaphor is hospitality. How we inhabit a space depends on how we imagine it. We recognize this truth in the way we arrange our rooms, our workplaces, and our houses. A quality distinguishing us from other animals, one that manifests our intelligence and imagination, is our penchant for changing the way we construct and arrange our dwelling places. The skyscraper, the motorized mobile home, the space capsule were nowhere to be seen a hundred years ago except in the imagination.[4]

People have inhabited the Earth itself differently according to the way they have imagined it. Centuries ago, our ancestors saw the Earth as a flat surface covered by a canopy that was pierced by intelligent stars and warmed by a sun traveling across it once a day. Later the Earth was imagined as a sphere rotating around the sun, and still later as one of many such spheres in one of billions of galaxies. There is more in these changing views than a development of scientific knowledge validated empirically. Myth and metaphor are also present, *myth* here meaning a set of beliefs for grasping complexity as a comprehensible whole, and *metaphor* as a figure of speech that stands for something else. Both myth and metaphor express an imaginative grasp of something that is beyond adequate analysis, beyond linear cause and effect thinking. To live creatively and nonviolently in the world today depends on imaginative ways of experiencing the world whole. New metaphors go hand in hand with imagination. We have such metaphors as the global village and Spaceship Earth, to mention two relatively recent metaphors that point to what we are searching for. Emerging now is a powerful metaphor based on the experience of hospitality, a way of seeing the Earth as dwelling place with strong overtones of home. This metaphor enables us to see humankind as homemakers, welcoming others, collaborating with others rather than competing with them, caring for one another and for the Earth as our common home.

The metaphor of home, with its overtones of hospitality, may be more powerful today than either global village or Spaceship Earth because home, better than either of the other two metaphors, expresses a needed affective quality associated with caring. To see our planet as our common home is to imagine the Earth not as a source of raw materials to be exploited for ourselves, but as a dwelling place to be continually tended for all who live here and for those to come after us. All together we are required to care for the air, water, soil, and all else that nourishes us. This includes our values, our history, and our best traditions. Homemaking is an ongoing art dependent on the quality of participation of all who share the living space. Seeing the Earth as home immediately makes the connection between nonviolence, ecology, social institutions, and culture.

The potential of home and hospitality for shifting our perspective on issues of economic and political security deserves careful consideration. The quest for adequate defense through military force has generated an arms race that is constantly spawning more lethal weaponry; the weaponry, in turn, has made the human family immensely more vulnerable. This suggests that those relying on the most advanced armaments are looking in the wrong direction in an effort to provide security. Rather than look to superior weaponry, to power from threats of punishment, we can direct our search toward seeing the world differently because it is different. A sign of readiness for the emergence of this shift is in the increasing recognition that national sovereignty is relative, not absolute. National sovereignty cannot be absolute in an increasingly globalized economy and a culture of near-instant communication. We can never again take state-provided security for granted.

To foster the practice of hospitality as a central theme of a spirituality of peace and nonviolence is one way to contribute to a culture in which we see ourselves primarily as artists called to create together a home for the human family, rather than primarily as citizens of a particular nation. However, we will not abandon our old loyalties as we transcend them. Of necessity, we will still have political institutions and nations and will prize our citizenship, but our first identification will be with the human family. Hospitality extended to the societal dimension of life makes this possible.

Hospitality is a distinctively human act toward another, a way of responding, of reaching out, of welcoming. It involves more than providing physical shelter. Animals make or find nests, hives, and dens for themselves and their young, and occasionally animals take care of young not their own. This is not hospitality as we understand the term. The difference is in the depths of the person touched by hospitality. We have all had the experience of hospitality when nothing material was offered. A welcoming smile offers hospitality because it comes straight from the heart and goes directly to the heart.

Martin Buber, in *I and Thou,* writes that all living is a meeting. What he means is that truly human living is experienced in a certain quality of encounter. In an I-thou relationship, persons meet each other as subjects present to each other, not as objects for each other's benefit. Hospitality is a mode of human interaction that certainly tends toward I-thou relationship and often reaches it. We do not experience the fullness of I-thou relationships at every encounter; however, every meeting with another should be influenced by the deepest reality in which we are grounded, namely, an I-thou relationship with God.

In hospitality we do not act as client or offer professional services; rather, we act as guest or host. Throughout our lives we are called to play both parts many times. When we play either role well, it brings out the best in us. The good host or hostess is attentive to the comfort, desire, and needs of guests. Guests, in turn, take care not to offend, to be aware of how much others do for their comfort, and to express sincere thanks. Both guests and hosts recognize a measure of vulnerability in the relationship.

A guest is at the mercy of someone else, probably by choice, but nevertheless really dependent. Ordinarily we are not conscious of vulnerability in a guest-host relationship because of another inherent quality: trust. Guest and host trust each other, expect with confidence that they are safe in each other's company. It is trust in others' goodness that makes all peaceful human relationships possible. Hospitality raises the level of trust in any community, and to that extent it is a service to the common good, to the quality of life of all of us. Without a single word, guest and host, by their entering into the relationship, say to each other that they honor the mystery of human dignity in each other.

The first act of the host is welcoming. Each time we have an opportunity to welcome another, whether a stranger or a member of our immediate family, we are offered the possibility of expressing God's gracious love. We keep that love alive in our own small world, and from there it radiates farther through our neighborhood and beyond. The act of warm welcoming speaks to us of the possibilities of human relationship to which we are faithfully called; it keeps alive the vision of the peaceable kingdom in which the wolf will be the guest of the lamb, the panther lie down with the kid, the calf and the lion cub feed together (Isa 11:6).

During the Great Depression of the 1930s, Dorothy Day and Peter Maurin began the Catholic Worker Movement, which from the beginning included houses of hospitality as a response clearly called for by the gospel. Catholic Worker houses continue to flourish today. The movement has always called its homes "houses of hospitality" rather than shelters for the homeless. Dorothy Day and Peter Maurin envisioned a day in which there would be a house of hospitality in each parish. Dorothy described the beginning of their first house of hospitality: "So far three beds are all that have been obtained although fifteen are needed. We also have four blankets, two of them donated by a woman, the members of whose family are unemployed, save for one son who is working for ten dollars a week....The winter is on us and we can wait no longer. Even without furniture we have opened the doors."[5]

On another occasion she wrote:

Part of the House of Hospitality has moved down to Easton. As we keep explaining, our idea of hospitality means that everyone with a home should have a guest room. Two women who help us with the paper and who are interested in our ideas have moved into tenement apartments on Mott Street and use their spare rooms for those in need of hospitality. One of the striking stewardesses is staying in one apartment, and another woman temporarily out of employment is staying with our friend in the other.[6]

Dorothy's idea of hospitality continued to develop. For her, hospitality was a normal and necessary expression of Christian faith. She wrote:

> We emphasize always the necessity of smallness. The ideal, of course, would be that each Christian, conscious of his duty...should take in one of the homeless as an honored guest, remembering Christ's words: "Inasmuch as ye have done it unto the least of these, ye have done it unto me." The poor are more conscious of this obligation than those who are comfortably off. I know any number of cases where families already overburdened and crowded, have taken in orphaned children, homeless aged, poor who were not members of their families but who were akin to them because they were fellow sufferers in this disordered world.[7]

Dorothy Day's deep wisdom is expressed in a single line of an old Gaelic saying: "It is in the shelter of each other that the people live." People are meant to live in no other way. Life flourishes or languishes in proportion to the quality of human relationships. It is in reciprocity of giving and receiving, in an ongoing flow of energy, in loving exchange that we discover and realize our human potential. Hospitality adds an affective dimension to this understanding and experience, rescuing it from cold reasoning devoid of emotion. Hospitality helps instill with moral power the principle and fact of interdependence. In his 1971 apostolic letter *A Call to Action,* Pope Paul VI wrote movingly of the need for hospitality, especially in poor urban areas:

> It is in fact the weakest who are the victims of dehumanizing living conditions, degrading for conscience and harmful for the family....The promiscuity of working people's

housing makes a minimum of intimacy impossible; young couples waiting in vain for a decent dwelling at a price they can afford are demoralized and their union can thereby even be endangered; youth escape from a home which is too confined and seek in the street compensations and companionships which cannot be supervised. It is the grave duty of those responsible to strive to control this process and to give it direction.

There is urgent need to remake at the level of the street, of the neighborhood,...the social fabric whereby people may be able to develop the needs of their personality. Centers of special interest and of culture must be created or developed at the community and parish levels with different forms of associations, recreational centers, and spiritual and community gatherings where the individual can escape from isolation and form anew fraternal relationships.[8]

Hospitality touches us at the core when we find ourselves at home with ourselves as well as with others. When we take the time to welcome ourselves to our center we do not enter an empty place; rather, we encounter God in whom we live and move and have our being. God encompasses us, is more vitally present than the air that fills our lungs and keeps us alive and breathing. The answer of God to our deepest longing, a longing we perhaps rarely allow ourselves to face, and even more rarely to muse upon, is intimate presence. God is more intimately present to each of us than we are to ourselves. When we are at home with God who wants to be at home with us, all else more easily finds its place. A medieval hymn, *"Veni, Sancte Spiritus* (Come, Holy Spirit),"* addresses the Spirit as *dulcis hospes animae* ("delightful guest of the soul"). Hospitality can help us get in touch with our mysterious reality and also with a way of understanding the meaning of nonviolence at this moment in human history. Welcoming God as our guest, we can also welcome one another with loving care and learn to make of our world a home for all who dwell here. It is in the attitude and practice of hospitality that we find a creative way of dealing with the many kinds of conflict that are an integral part of life.

Nonviolence and Conflict

Nonviolence is most needed and too often absent in situations of conflict. Dictionaries define *conflict* as (1) competitive or opposing action of incompatibles; (2) antagonistic states or actions; and (3) mental struggles resulting from incompatible or opposing needs, drives, wishes, or external or internal demands. These definitions can include hostile encounters, fights, battles, and wars. We can verify all these definitions from experience, identifying conflicts on three levels: within ourselves, between and among persons, and large-scale conflicts that may be political, economic, military, or all of these at once.

Today the study of conflict and ways of dealing with it questions the notion that conflict is always and only bad. A conflict may be a valuable opportunity for developing abilities that would otherwise remain unrecognized and undeveloped. We regularly deal with some conflicts not by resolving them once and for all but by managing them, recognizing that these conflicts are not necessarily bad but that our way of dealing with them may need improvement or even change. Examples include the conflict between desire for food and weight control, between the need for sleep and the desire for activities that cut into needed rest, between the need for socializing and the need for solitude. Successfully managing these ongoing conflicts contributes not only to the maintenance of physical health but also to the development of character.

Serious conflicts between two or more persons may require resolution rather than ongoing management. These conflicts provide us with many of our opportunities for personal growth. When interpersonal conflicts are not managed well or resolved, that is, brought to some healthy closure, they can poison or destroy what were once most cherished relationships with spouses, children, friends, neighbors, and professional colleagues and associates. Today conflict resolution is recognized as a profession answering to a widespread human need. A growing number of universities offer graduate-level programs in conflict resolution.

The search for alternatives to violence, and especially to the violence of war, is a frontier of research engaging more and more people. War is a particular kind of conflict that involves the legalized killing of enemies in the social organization of killing, mostly of persons who are not combatants. The deadly conflict of wars between and within states killed more than a hundred million persons in the twentieth century, more than twelve times those killed in all wars in the nineteenth century. This statistic explains in part the urgency to find ways to deal constructively with war as a particular kind of conflict. The devastation of war goes far beyond the number of persons directly killed. War leaves in its wake wrecked lives and families and a legacy of bitterness that all too easily becomes the seedbed for another war in an ever-escalating spiral of violence.

The resolution of a conflict and the means to achieve the resolution are integrally related. Gandhi said that the end is contained in the means. War may put a halt to a conflict in the short run by inflicting an unacceptable level of pain on an enemy, but this is certainly not a good resolution for either side. History demonstrates that even the reluctant acceptance of war, as a "necessary evil" or as a "just war," is part of a spiral that seeks always for more effective ways to win by inflicting unacceptable levels of damage on the enemy until the enemy surrenders. The logic of war has brought us to the point at which nuclear weapons for prevailing in war are produced and stockpiled as a threat of unimaginable proportions, although they are morally unusable. More than ever before in human history, the most beautiful victories will be the wars we do not fight. Put another way, the best way to deal with a war is to prevent it by substituting win-win strategies for win-lose contests of strength. A conflict thus transformed leaves all parties better off than before.

How can conflicts be transformed from win-lose contests to win-win contests? Such transformation depends on one's view of the human person, as well as on a sense of timing and on a set of practices that can properly be called an art. Conflict-transforming strategies require the ability to see a conflict not as opposing action of incompatibles, in which one side wins and the other side loses, but as a common problem to be solved. All this is taught in a growing number of universities throughout the world in departments and programs of peace and conflict studies. Outside academia there are other venues where one can learn ways to deal with conflict without inflicting damage on either party. Transformation needs more than academic peace studies, however; it also requires a level of professional practice akin to an internship.

While much is known about nonviolent approaches and win-win strategies for dealing with small-scale conflicts in personal and professional relationships, today there are also an increasing number of well-documented examples of such efforts on a large scale.[9] The documentation of examples where nonviolence has worked is a challenge to historians. National histories conventionally emphasize wars in which the accent is on military heroism and also on a distortion of the real causes that foment wars. The best that can be concluded from most historical treatments of war is that it seems to be a necessary evil in which some make the supreme sacrifice for the sake of their country. Both sides see the other side as causing the war. One has only to study a major war from the accounts of two opposing sides to confirm the well-founded suspicion that the first casualty in any war is the truth.

A transformational approach to war as a special kind of conflict is based on the premise that war is an unnecessary evil. Such an approach engages human capacities that may well be latent or underdeveloped. Among these are creative imagination and compassion. A peace studies curriculum that develops into a peace service curriculum, including an internship, will place a strong emphasis on these powers, among others.

Those seeking to transform a win-lose conflict, whether between individuals or between states, hold as a first principle a concern for the well-being of all parties. This is a tall order, of course, and explains why compassionate listening and benevolent glancing as described in the previous chapter are relevant practices in dealing with all kinds of conflicts. Win-win methods are really expressions of love. We all know when we experience this kind of love in ourselves or witness it in a heroic degree in others. Every human being can grow in this fundamental posture and practice throughout life. What we are beginning to realize, one hopes, is that love is now a necessity for survival as it never has been before. W. H. Auden, writing at the beginning of World War II, correctly observed, "We must love one another or die."[10] Roger Fischer and William Ury of the Harvard Negotiating Project, authors of *Getting to Yes: Negotiating Agreement without Giving In*, explain that for successful win-win conflict management or resolution, at least one side must have a desire for what is needed by the other side. This, of course, requires knowing what is needed. According to the authors, the universal basic needs are five: security, economic well-being, a sense of belonging, recognition, and some measure of control over one's life. Some measure of control over one's life includes participation in decisions seriously affecting one's life.[11] To this list I would add the need to take risks, both as a requirement for dealing with conflict constructively and for a person's own development of character. Without acknowledging the need for risk taking, too much emphasis is put on the need for security and for economic well-being. It is in recognizing a set of needs that constructive approaches to conflict are discovered or invented, and risk taking is integral to the set.

Few of us act directly as combatants in large-scale conflicts, but more and more we are involved in large conflicts as supporters or victims, even if unwittingly and indirectly. We may become actors in conflicts simply by being citizens of a particular nation at a particular time. This is a consequence of globalization of the economy that is making us increasingly interdependent. As never before we are faced with the consequences of the fact that the old methods of winning through military force have led from the club to the nuclear weapon and beyond, and now to the growing fear of terrorism with biological and chemical weapons. This situation persists because society at large aids and abets it or at least tolerates it. That is one good reason for learning to manage, resolve, and transform conflicts well in our own small worlds. All our small worlds are connected to the larger arenas. Today this is of crucial importance because the very survival of our life-sustaining planet is threatened by life-threatening ways and by weapons of mass destruction that must be abolished, but will not be abolished until our culture and society rely on alternative ways to satisfy the fundamental need for security.

In such a culture and such a society, tested methods for teaching nonviolent conflict resolution and management and transformation will be part of a curriculum in many colleges, universities, and other places of adult education. The foundation will be laid earlier in elementary and secondary education. Many people will learn how to anticipate and prevent conflicts and how to map them, identifying the needs and also the fears and anxieties of participants in conflicts. They will also learn courageously to face injustices that are at the root of many if not all conflicts;

and they will do this knowing that they are helping to make a home of our global village.

QUESTIONS FOR STUDY, REFLECTION, AND CONVERSATION

1. A good place to practice nonviolence is in our daily speaking. Give examples.
2. Why is war prevention more urgent than ever before? Alone, or preferably with others, draw up a list of ways of war prevention. Then discuss which of these ways (a) can be put into practice now, (b) require specialized training and support, (c) should be goals of public policy.
3. Why is it urgent to experiment with alternatives to war? Can you imagine some of the elements of alternatives to armed conflict?
4. Give some examples to illustrate the meaning of the Gaelic saying, "It is in the shelter of each other that the people live."
5. How do you understand the relationship between hospitality and nonviolence? Give examples of this relationship at various levels of human encounter: (a) interpersonal, (b) at the level of the local civic community, (c) at the national level, (d) between or among several nations, (e) globally.
6. Explain how "violence may be in the form of economic and social injustice as well as armed violence" (p. 49).
7. Give examples of (a) conflict management, (b) conflict resolution, (c) conflict transformation.

NOTES

1. J. Glenn Gray, *The Warriors: Reflections on Men in Battle* (New York: Harper and Row, 1970). See especially chapter 2, "The Enduring Appeals of Battle."

2. A systematic study of Gandhi is indispensable for understanding modern nonviolence. Among the hundreds of available titles, the following books read in order provide an introduction: a biography, for example, Louis Fischer, *Gandhi: His Life and Message for the World* (New York: Signet, 1989); or Eknath Easwaran, *Gandhi, the Man: The Story of His Transformation* (Tomales, CA: Nilgiri Press, 1997). Two sources of Gandhi's writings are his (partial) autobiography written in prison, *An Autobiography: The Story of My Experiments*

with Truth (Boston: Beacon Press, 1993); and *Autobiographical Reflections* (New York: Continuum, 1980). A fine account and analysis of some of his nonviolent campaigns is Joan V. Bondurant, *Conquest of Violence: The Gandhian Philosophy of Conflict* (Princeton, NJ: Princeton University Press, 1988).

3. Milton Mayeroff, *On Caring* (New York: Harper and Row, 1971). In chapter 2, Mayeroff considers the "major ingredients of caring": knowing, alternating rhythms, patience, honesty, trust, humility, hope, and courage as these are practiced in caring for people but also in caring for ideas.

4. See Gibson Winter on paradigms of human dwelling, in *Liberating Creation: Foundations of Religious Social Ethics* (New York: Crossroad, 1981), 37–44; and Michael J. Himes on imagination, in *Doing the Truth in Love: Conversations about God, Relationships and Service* (New York/Mahwah, NJ: Paulist Press, 1995), 136–38.

5. Dorothy Day, *Meditations,* selected and edited by Stanley Vishnewski (New York: Paulist Press, 1970), 15–16.

6. Ibid., 33.

7. Ibid.

8. *Octogesima Adveniens,* art. 11, p. 269, in David J. O'Brien and Thomas A. Shannon, eds., *Catholic Social Thought: The Documentary Heritage* (Maryknoll, NY: Orbis, 1992).

9. Richard Deats, "The Global Spread of Active Nonviolence," in Walter Wink, ed., *Peace Is the Way: Writings on Nonviolence from the Fellowship of Reconciliation* (Maryknoll, NY: Orbis, 2000), 283–95.

10. W. H. Auden, "September 1, 1939," in W. H. Auden, *Selected Poems, New Edition,* ed. Edward Mendelson (New York: Vintage Books, 1979), 88.

11. Roger Fisher and William Ury, *Getting to Yes: Negotiating Agreement without Giving In* (New York: Penguin Books, 1981), 50.

CHAPTER FIVE

Effective Learning

Speaking the truth in love, we must grow up in every way into him who is the head, into Christ.
—Ephesians 4:15

CHAPTER FOCUS

Catholic social teaching has made it increasingly clear that action on behalf of justice is a constitutive part of the preaching of the gospel, that is, of the church's mission for the redemption of the world. The effectiveness of social action depends on the quality of our learning, a process that often includes reading, reflection, discussion, and writing that leads to further action. Human experience is the starting point for much theological learning, and within that experience, the signs of the times require careful scrutiny.

Introduction

If you have read this far, you probably hope to find in this book some help in living and working more effectively for a more just and peaceful world, at least the world of your local community. Although we know that things don't get better through indifference and neglect, we may often feel that there is little we can do in the face of complex issues of social injustice and violence. This chapter and the next aim to provide some modest means of participating in work for justice and peace in solidarity with people of good will throughout the world. While this entire book is intended to help the reader integrate prayer, learning, and action for social change, this chapter and the next focus on effective ways of learning. As we shall see, this involves much more than acquiring information.

A Learning Rhythm

Learning is effective when it stimulates change in ourselves and change in our society. The sixteenth-century writer Francis Bacon captured the basic elements of an effective learning rhythm: "Reading maketh a full man, conference a ready man, writing an exact man."[1] If Francis Bacon were writing today he might well have said it this way: Reading or listening makes a well-informed person, discussion an articulate person, and writing an exact person. This description leaves out one essential step: reflection. We need to reflect well about what we have read or heard before we discuss it. Likewise, after discussion we need to reflect again before we write. Reflection makes a thoughtful and insightful person. Reflection is also a necessary ingredient of wise expression, whether oral or written. When we reflect, we can compare what we have learned with our experience, make connections, analyze data, identify gaps in our knowledge, and envision new possibilities. Sometimes reflection stirs our emotions and imagination and raises further questions, while at other times it gives us a fresh insight. Reflection moves us to action. We also acquire the strength to persevere or in some cases change our actions when we cultivate a habit of reflection on the consequences of these actions.

So, we can now revise Bacon's saying to read: Reading and listening make a well-informed person, reflection a thoughtful and insightful person, discussion an articulate person, and writing an exact person. This method assumes that we do not delude ourselves into thinking that we automatically take time for reflection just because we recognize its importance; rather, whatever the demands on our lives, we need to safeguard time and space for regular reflection. In this learning rhythm, writing also needs some affirmative action. Writing here implies much more than taking notes while listening or reading: writing that "makes an exact mind" is reflective writing.

To keep a journal of this kind of writing, to set aside quality time at regular intervals to do it, is a discipline that can make all the difference in the quality of our learning and in the lasting effect it will have in our lives. When we write reflectively, we are able to name what we are learning and can identify the next questions we want to explore. We can also discover the blocks to our learning and gaps in what we are trying to master. Unless we write, even our best ideas may slip away from us. Figure 1 summarizes this learning rhythm.

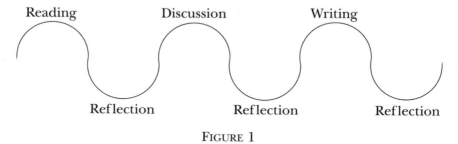

Reading   Discussion   Writing

Reflection   Reflection   Reflection

FIGURE 1

Turn to the Human

We turn now to the theological framework in which we pray, study, and act. Catholic social teaching, which has developed remarkably since 1891, falls within the broader field of moral theology and is an important source for our theological reflection. Moral theology is the study of human activity in the context of the human relationship to God. The quality of moral theology depends on its relationship to the totality of theology, that is, to our understanding of the mystery of God and the mystery of the church and the sacraments. If moral theology is taken out of this rich context, it can degenerate into a dismal legalism, to a narrow focus on what is morally permissible or not permissible.

For centuries, moral theology began with principles and applied or tested them against what was seen as unchanging, timeless human nature. This resulted in a moral theology that emphasized laws and sin—hardly an inspiration for a dynamic Christian life. In the second half of the twentieth century, Catholic moral theologians changed their methods of studying and teaching in ways that can accurately be called revolutionary. This radical change involves a new starting place for theological reflection. The new starting place is not some abstract human nature but the human person. Human nature and natural law are still useful ideas in moral theology, but they have a more nuanced meaning, a different weight. This shift in theological method is called the "turn to the subject," that is, to the human person; it is sometimes called the "anthropological turn," or the "turn to the human." It has been influenced by the development of the sciences—including psychology, sociology, economics, and anthropology—that are called "human sciences" because their field of inquiry is precisely some aspect of human activity.

The turn to the human has deeply influenced Catholic social teaching and Catholic social thought since the mid-twentieth century. The Second Vatican Council's *Pastoral Constitution on the Church in the Modern World* exemplifies the shift in a number of ways: in its treatment of the dignity of the human person in part I, and in devoting a chapter each to the proper development of culture, socioeconomic life, and the life of the political community in part II. The opening lines are magisterial in announcing the way the church intended to approach its theological teaching about the church in the modern world:

> The joys and the hopes, the griefs and the anxieties of the men [people] of this age, especially those who are poor or in any way afflicted, these, too, are the joys and hopes, the griefs and anxieties of the followers of Christ. Indeed, nothing genuinely human fails to raise an echo in their hearts. For theirs is a community composed of men [people]. United in Christ, they are led by the Holy Spirit in their journey to the kingdom of their Father and they have welcomed the news of salvation which is meant for every man [person]. That is why this community realizes that it is truly and intimately linked with mankind [humankind] and its history.[2]

The Pastoral Constitution on the Church in the Modern World, the last of the council documents to be completed, benefits from the theological riches of the council, especially its renewed and deepened understanding of the church itself. This document confidently offers to the entire human family its reflections on contemporary social realities:

> Hence this Second Vatican Council, having probed more profoundly into the mystery of the Church, now addresses

itself without hesitation, not only to the sons [and daugh-
ters] of the Church and to all who invoke the name of
Christ, but to the whole of humanity. For the Council
yearns to explain to everyone how it conceives of the presence and activity of the Church in the world of today.

Therefore, the Council focuses its attention on the
world of men [and women], the whole human family along
with the sum of those realities in the midst of which that
family lives. It gazes on that world which is the theater of
man's [humankind's] history, and carries the marks of his
[its] energies, its tragedies, and its triumphs; that world
which the Christian sees as created and sustained by its
Maker's love, fallen indeed into the bondage of sin, yet
emancipated now by Christ. He was crucified and rose
again to break the stranglehold of personified Evil, so that
this world might be fashioned anew according to God's
design and reach its fulfillment.[3]

For the human person deserves to be preserved; human
society deserves to be renewed. Hence the pivotal point of
our total presentation will be man himself [the human per-
son], whole and entire, body and soul, heart and conscience, mind and will.

Therefore, this sacred synod proclaims the highest destiny of man [the human person] and champions the god-
like seed which has been sown in him [them]. It offers to
mankind [humankind] the honest assistance of the church
in fostering that brotherhood [communion] of all people
which corresponds to this destiny of theirs.[4]

Another good example of the turn to the human is the 1971
Roman Synod of Bishops. This representative group of bishops
took up the topic of justice in the world, and after several weeks
of discussion, together with Pope Paul VI they issued a pastoral
document, *Justice in the World,* to the entire church. Early in the
document they say:

The world in which the Church lives and acts is held cap-
tive by a tremendous paradox. Never before have the
forces working for bringing about a unified world society
appeared so powerful and dynamic; they are rooted in the
awareness of the full basic equality as well as of the human

dignity of all. Since men [and women] are members of the same human family, they are indissolubly linked with one another in the one destiny of the whole world, in the responsibility for which they all share.

The paradox lies in the fact that within this perspective of unity the forces of division and antagonism seem today to be increasing in strength....Unless combated and overcome by social and political action, the influence of the new industrial and technological order favors the concentration of wealth, power and decision-making in the hands of a small public or private controlling group. Economic injustice and lack of social participation keep people from attaining their basic human and civil rights.[5]

Moral theologian Richard McCormick, SJ, in his book *Creative Vision,* writes of the effect the turn to the human has had on theology:

Moral theologians today are much more aware of the need of sound theological anthropology. By "theological anthropology" I mean a doctrine of the human person that views the human person in terms of the great Christian mysteries: creation-fall-redemption. It is a doctrine that would yield an appropriate emphasis on vision, perspectives, and character, and the stories, metaphors and images that generate and nourish these elements. Vatican II summarized this very cryptically: "Faith throws a new light on everything, manifests God's design for man's total vocation, and thus directs the mind to solutions which are fully human." The terms "God's design" and "total vocation" are shorthand for theological anthropology.[6]

Reading the Signs of the Times

Reading the signs of the times is a specific application of the turn to the human in theological method. It marks a watershed in Catholic social teaching, both as a body of writing and as applied by Catholics in their day-to-day living. The terminology "signs of the times" is biblical (Matt 26:4), but its application in contemporary theological method began with Pope John XXIII. He used the phrase in the encyclical *Peace on Earth* (1963) to describe characteristics of contemporary culture and society considered especially significant in the human aspiration for peace through justice. Earlier social encyclicals addressed particular problems in society, but precisely as problems, not as signs in the way that has characterized Catholic social teaching since Pope John XXIII.

Pope John's use of signs of the times marks a shift of accent in theological reflection. Reading the signs of the times is based on the assumption that God reveals through events and their contexts. The signs of the times specified in *Peace on Earth* are found at the end of each of four chapters of the encyclical. They are presented here:

- Workers' rising consciousness of their dignity (art. 40)
- Women's rising consciousness of their dignity (art. 41)
- The end of colonialism; the aspiration to universal citizenship based on rights and duties (arts. 42–45)
- Charters of human rights (art. 75)
- Written constitutions (arts. 76–78)
- Claims to political participation (art. 79)
- A growing awareness that disputes between states should not be solved by arms but by negotiations (arts. 126–29)
- The United Nations organization (arts. 141–42, 145)
- The Universal Declaration of Human Rights (arts. 143–44)

Reading the signs of the times was affirmed as a fundamental approach in *The Pastoral Constitution on the Church in the Modern World.* The introductory section makes this very clear:

Inspired by no earthly ambition, the Church seeks but a solitary goal: to carry forward the work of Christ himself under the lead of the befriending Spirit. And Christ entered this world to give witness to the truth, to rescue and not to sit in judgment, to serve and not to be served.

To carry out such a task, the Church has always had the duty of scrutinizing the signs of the times and of interpreting them in the light of the gospel....We must therefore recognize and understand the world in which we live, its expectations, its longings, and its often dramatic characteristics.[7]

The Pastoral Constitution then describes a number of these characteristics in considerable detail. For example:

> Never has the human race enjoyed such an abundance of wealth, resources, and economic power. Yet a huge proportion of the world's citizens is still tormented by hunger and poverty, while countless numbers suffer from total illiteracy. Never before today has man [have people] been so keenly aware of freedom, yet at the same time, new forms of social and psychological slavery make their appearance.
>
> Although the world of today has a very vivid sense of its unity and of how one man [person] depends on another in needful solidarity, it is most grievously torn into opposing camps by conflicting forces. For political, social, economic, racial, and ideological disputes still continue bitterly, and with them the peril of a war which would reduce everything to ashes.[8]

What, precisely, distinguishes a sign of the times from other signs? First, a sign of the times must be a widespread phenomenon, a notable change from a previously prevailing situation, or at least it must be a condition that is freshly perceived as urgent. However, this is not sufficient. A widespread technological advance, for example, is not necessarily a sign of the times. Only when a widespread social change or perception is in tension with a prevailing cultural norm or moral norm does it constitute a genuine sign of the times.

The following two descriptions of signs of the times in *Peace on Earth* make this clear:

> It is obvious to everyone that women are now taking part in public life. This is happening more rapidly perhaps in nations of Christian civilization, and, more slowly, but broadly, among peoples who have inherited other traditions or cultures. Since women are becoming ever more conscious of their human dignity, they will not tolerate being treated as mere material instruments, but demand

rights befitting a human person both in domestic and in public life. (art. 41)

Men [people] are becoming more and more convinced that disputes which arise between states should not be resolved by recourse to arms, but rather by negotiation. We grant indeed that this conviction is chiefly based on the terrible destructive force of modern weapons and a fear of the calamities and frightful destruction which such weapons would cause. Therefore, in an age such as ours which prides itself on its atomic energy it is contrary to reason to hold that war is now a suitable way to restore rights which have been violated. (arts. 126–27)[9]

The appeal to read the signs of the times was continued by Pope Paul VI in the apostolic letter *A Call to Action* (1971) and in the apostolic exhortation, *Evangelization in the Modern World* (1975). The Synod document, *Justice in the World* (1971), begins by calling attention to what had by then become a prominent theological method:

Scrutinizing the "signs of the times" and seeking to detect the meaning of emerging history, while at the same time sharing the aspirations and questionings of all those who want to build a more human world, we have listened to the Word of God that we might be converted to the fulfilling of the divine plan for the salvation of the world.[10]

Justice in the World differs noticeably from *Peace on Earth* in one respect: Where John emphasized positive developments while recognizing that they create tension because they challenge the status quo, *Justice in the World* is more explicit about negative as well as positive signs:

Even though it is not for us to elaborate a very profound analysis of the situation of the world, we have nevertheless been able to perceive the serious injustices which are building around the world of men [people] a network of domination, oppression, and abuses which stifle freedom and which keep the greater part of humanity from sharing in the building up and enjoyment of a more just and more fraternal world.

At the same time we have noted the inmost stirring moving the world in its depths. There are facts constituting a contribution to the furthering of justice. In associations of men [and women] and among people themselves there is arising a new awareness which shakes them out of any fatalistic resignation and which spurs them on to liberate themselves and to be responsible for their own destiny. Movements among men [people] are seen which express hope in a better world and a will to change whatever has become intolerable.

Listening to the cry of those who suffer violence and are oppressed by unjust systems and structures, and hearing the appeal of a world that by its perversity contradicts the plan of its Creator, we have shared our awareness of the Church's vocation to be present in the heart of the world by proclaiming the Good News to the poor, freedom to the oppressed, and joy to the afflicted. The hopes and forces which are moving the world in its very foundations are not foreign to the dynamism of the Gospel, which through the power of the Holy Spirit frees men [people] from personal sin and from its consequences in social life.[11]

The next paragraph gives the conclusion that the bishops drew from this description. The final sentence is the most quoted passage of *Justice in the World:*

The uncertainty of history and the painful convergences in the ascending path of the human community direct us to sacred history; there God has revealed himself to us, and made known to us, as it is brought progressively to realization, his plan of liberation and salvation which is once and for all fulfilled in the Paschal Mystery of Christ. Action on behalf of justice and participation in the transformation of the world fully appear to us as a constitutive dimension of the preaching of the Gospel, or, in other words, of the Church's mission for the redemption of the human race and its liberation from every oppressive situation.[12]

This passage draws a profound theological conclusion from a reflection on specific signs of the times. It suggests that a sign of the times may be a social situation that involves pain and conflict but that also allows for a profound creative and redeeming movement of the Holy Spirit in those who discern in faith a revelation of God in human affairs.

Doing the Truth in Love

In 1975, Pope Paul VI singled out signs of the times especially significant for the mission of the church. He wrote:

> It is often said nowadays that the present century thirsts for authenticity. Especially in regard to young people it is said that they have a horror of the artificial or false and that they are searching above all for truth and honesty. These "signs of the times" should find us vigilant. Either tacitly or aloud—but always forcefully—we are being asked: Do you really believe what you are proclaiming? Do you live what you believe? Do you really preach what you live? The witness of life has become more than ever an essential condition for real effectiveness in preaching. Precisely because of this we are, to a certain extent, responsible for the progress of the Gospel that we proclaim.[13]

Here the pope is writing about a faith that is more than an intellectual assent to truths that God has revealed. Certainly there is an essential component of intellectual assent in an act of faith, but the acid test of genuine faith is in the actions that flow from that faith. The teaching of Paul VI echoes that found in the New Testament:

> What good is it, my brothers, if someone says he has faith but does not have works? Can that faith save him? If a brother or sister has nothing to wear and has no food for the day, and one of you says to them, "Go in peace, keep warm, and eat well," but you do not give them the necessities of the body, what good is it? So also faith of itself, if it does not have works, is dead. Indeed, someone might say, "You have faith and I have works." Demonstrate your faith to me without works, and I will demonstrate my faith to you from my works. (Jas 2:14–18)

Besides intellectual assent, faith that expresses itself in action includes a strong element of trust. Trust enables us to exchange confidence in our own strength and ideas for confidence in the power and guiding word of another. In Christian faith, our trust is in God. Christians know God in Jesus Christ as we experience him in community. This is the profound mystery of faith. Christian faith is possible for us because it has been handed down in the communion of saints we call the church. The communion of saints is also a communion of sinners who know that they are loved.

The church can be understood as a two-thousand-year response to the life and teaching of Jesus, in whom words and actions were completely consistent. Jesus' trust in God expressed itself in the complete gift of himself. The power of the church is the power to remember Jesus Christ and to act on that memory. One of the church's most powerful memories is Jesus' story in the Gospel of Matthew, chapter 25:31–45, which describes the great divide between those who came to the aid of those in dire need and those who did not. There is no middle ground, and on both sides the judged are surprised when informed, "I was hungry and you gave me food"...or, "I was hungry and you gave me no food." This story is compelling not so much as a moral exhortation but because it enlightens us about the meaning of our lives as we go about our daily round. In this parable, Jesus says that we are protagonists in a divine drama, not a stage play but the real thing. What is at stake here is the central question of Catholic social teaching. How are we to live out this teaching of the gospel that human destiny is inseparable from a divine reality, that God, having become fully human in Jesus, is closer to us by faith than anything we can see? What difference does two thousand years of history make, a history that is not a repetition of earlier events, but a story of increasing human penetration of the working of the world, of triumphs and failure not only of individuals but of entire civilizations?

The Second Vatican Council labored to answer these questions, and all subsequent Catholic social teaching has continued that effort. In Catholic social teaching, active faith that expresses itself in good works extends beyond acts directed toward individuals to issues that affect social structures. In chapters 7 to 10 we shall see the application of this principle. Before that, chapter 6 continues an exploration of a theological foundation for transforming action.

QUESTIONS FOR STUDY, REFLECTION, AND CONVERSATION

1. From your own experience, describe how something you learned brought about a change in the way you act.
2. In which of the four skills of learning do you need most practice? Make a plan to improve this skill.
3. What is your starting point in making moral decisions? Where do you look for guidance?
4. Make a short list of the joys, hopes, griefs, and anxieties of the people of the world today. Which ones move you deeply? What responses do you make? Are you open to further response? What are obstacles to a fuller response?
5. Give examples of the paradox described by the 1971 Synod of Bishops in Rome.
6. What distinguishes signs of the times from other signs?
7. Of the signs of the times identified by Pope John XXIII in the encyclical *Pacem in Terris,* which ones are close to your own experience? Can you suggest signs of the times that Pope John would probably add if he were writing *Pacem in Terris* today?
8. Read, reflect, discuss, and write an essay on the statement of the 1971 Roman Synod on *Justice in the World*: "Action on behalf of justice and participation in the transformation of the world fully appear to us as a constitutive dimension of the preaching of the Gospel, or, in other words, of the Church's mission for the redemption of the human race and its liberation from every oppressive situation."
9. Comment on the following statement from page 73: "The power of the church is the power to remember Jesus Christ and to act on that memory."

NOTES

1. Francis Bacon, "Of Studies," in *The Essays or Counsels, Civil and Moral, of Francis Ld. Verulam Viscount St. Albans* (Mount Vernon, NY: Peter Pauper Press, n.d.), 196.

2. *Gaudium et Spes,* art. 1, p. 166, in David J. O'Brien and Thomas A. Shannon, eds., *Catholic Social Thought: The Documentary Heritage* (Maryknoll, NY: Orbis, 1992).

3. Ibid., art. 2, p. 166.

4. Ibid., art. 3, p. 167.

5. *Justice in the World*, 289, in O'Brien and Shannon, *Catholic Social Thought*.

6. Richard A. McCormick, SJ, *Corrective Vision: Explorations in Moral Theology* (Kansas City, MO: Sheed and Ward, 1994), 21.

7. *Gaudium et Spes*, arts. 3–4, p. 167.

8. Ibid., art. 4, p. 168.

9. *Pacem in Terris*, arts. 42, 126–27, pp. 137, 151, in O'Brien and Shannon, *Catholic Social Thought*.

10. *Justice in the World*, 288.

11. Ibid.

12. Ibid., 288–89.

13. *Evangelii Nuntiandi*, art. 76, p. 336, in O'Brien and Shannon, *Catholic Social Thought*.

CHAPTER SIX

— ⚜ —

Effective Action

[It is Christ,] from whom the whole body, joined and knit
together by every ligament with which it is equipped, as each
part is working properly, promotes the body's growth in
building itself up in love.
—Ephesians 4:16

CHAPTER FOCUS

Values can be correctly understood as both subjective and objective. The clarity of our values is a determining factor in the formation of character, for good or ill. Clarifying values involves choosing from alternatives, reflecting on these choices, experiencing peace with good choices even when they are very difficult, being able to explain choices, and acting on these choices with consistency. Bernard Lonergan developed an approach to learning that is completed in action, in a series of interior dynamic commands or transcendental imperatives: Be attentive, be understanding, be reasonable, be responsible, and be in love. Following these imperatives can be viewed as conversions: intellectual conversion (be attentive, understanding, reasonable); moral conversion (be responsible); and religious conversion (be in love). Clarifying one's values and following the transcendental imperatives can help us understand the relationship between effective learning and effective action on behalf of justice and peace.

The Meaning of Values

We are dynamic beings, and at the deepest core of our lives we experience a call to grow. Whether or not we reflect on it, we want to grow in knowledge and understanding, and we especially want to grow in loving relationships, because it is on these that our happiness depends. This is our call. How can we know if we are following it? How can we stay on our true path? The answer to these questions depends on what we value.

Value, in ordinary usage, means "worth," or "what a thing means to us."[1] This suggests that a thing has value according to the way we think about it at a given moment. For example, before Christmas, advertising may induce so great a desire for a particular toy that adults will pay a high price to obtain that toy for a child. A few years later, the same toy can be bought in a garage sale for a fraction of its original price. The worth of the toy has changed in the eyes of the child who had its heart set on it shortly before. We say that the toy has lost its value. When we talk about values in this way, we are talking about values as *subjective.* A subjective value is whatever a person wants. However, there are things of worth or value that are valuable in themselves, no matter what a particular individual thinks of them. A human life, a marriage, health, reputation, friendship—the worth or value of such goods is immeasurable and quite literally priceless. These are *objective* values. Such goods do not get their worth or value from personal opinion or from supply and demand. Objective values have value or worth whether we recognize it or not. When a person does prize an objective value, it becomes subjective only in the sense that the person, who here is the subject, makes it his or her own personal value.

As we continue our exploration into effective ways of learning that lead to action, we want to keep in mind an important relationship between these two commonly held notions of value, value as subjective, and value as objectively good. To the extent that persons are clear about their values, they express themselves effectively, act decisively, and influence others. Such persons exert leadership. Leaders for good and leaders for bad are both clear about their subjective values. Examples that come readily to mind are Adolf Hitler and Martin Luther King Jr. Hitler was clear about what he valued, and he laid out his values in speeches and in writing. They were certainly not objectively good values; they led to aggressive war and genocide. In contrast, Martin Luther King was clear about the value of a beloved community inclusive of all on the basis of human dignity and equal human rights. These were objectively good values, and they were also his own personal or subjective values. He was able to speak and write about them with great clarity. As a result he exerted extraordinary leadership in the nonviolent struggle for civil rights. He found ways to help others make these true values their own and to work together to make these the values of the wider society.

When people are not clear about their own deepest values, they tend to follow others uncritically. This is what gives advertising and propaganda incredible power. Many people buy what advertising persuades them to buy whether or not it is good for them, and they do what they are told to do without actively and reflectively choosing their actions. With a little help from propaganda, governments can ordinarily count on a submissive following. In obeying governments or military leaders, it may well be that a person values security too much and the common good too little. Those who value security at any price will do almost anything the government tells them to do.

In our daily lives we operate with these two notions of value: (1) value as something we hold dear, something on which we base important decisions; and (2) value as something that has worth in itself, whether or not we prize it personally. The first notion of value is subjective and may apply to something that has little intrinsic worth, such as the toy in the previous example. This first sense of value can also apply in serious decisions, and not necessarily positively. A person may value the pleasure of smoking more than health, for example. In this case a subjective value, the pleasure of smoking, is contrary to an objective value, health. Values are acquired by personal effort. They are not given to us, even by our parents, teachers, or any other significant persons in our lives. These people and others can, however, influence the formation of our values. They do this primarily by example, but also by teaching.

The answer to two questions about values will have a defining effect on our personal development and on the way we go about working for social change: (1) Do I value what is truly good? (2) How can I know that I actually value something that I recognize as truly good? It is important to remember that while the word *value* ordinarily stands for what is truly good, a person or a group can cling to what is morally bad and consider it valuable. It is this clinging, this pernicious attachment, that gives evil such power on the societal level. Such evils as economic discrimination based on race or gender, or atrocities of war, are not accidental; they are logical expressions of warped values embedded in the culture and institutions of a society.

Learning to Clarify Values

I can learn to clarify my values by systematically reflecting on what I think are my most deeply cherished values. The first step is to name something I think of as a value, something that I hold dear, and that I use as the basis for decisions. The value I name is of genuine importance, and named in a concrete, descriptive way. For example, "I value being a friend and having friends, particularly _____." In contrast, "I value friendship" is a statement of an abstract principle. In the second step, I ask myself if I chose this value from alternatives; or, is it something that I think is valuable but which has never been a matter of choice over some other good that I also hold dear? For example, do I take time for a friend when it means giving up something else that I really want to do?

The third step in clarifying a value is perhaps the most important, the most exacting, and the most neglected. In this step I reflect on my choice, its motives, and the consequences of my choice. I also reflect on what the consequences might have been had I made a different choice. This is the habit of reflection discussed at the beginning of chapter 5. There it was applied to learning about reality outside ourselves. Here reflection is turned to personal values that are the wellsprings of action.

In the fourth step, I try to get in touch with my feelings, and particularly with the experience of peace or its absence. When I make my own a value that is objectively good, I experience peace even if I cannot define the word, and even if the value choice I made involved difficulty or pain. I should also be able to explain my value choice if the situation calls for it. In the example of valuing a friendship with a particular person, I should be able to explain why this friendship is valuable.

Finally, I ask myself if I have *acted* on my value choice or whether it is still only a goal, a desire, or an ideal to be acted upon. Have I acted consistently? One act expressing an ideal or a principle is not enough to establish a value, which is a stable character trait. However, I am not to be surprised or discouraged if I discover that I cannot answer a firm "Yes" to all the tests implied in these questions. Ideals, strong desires, thoughtful resolutions are all *value indicators* that show a direction I am taking. Values are hard earned, and many times what I thought was a value may very well have been just such a value indicator. Besides ideals, strong desires, and thoughtful resolutions, value indicators include aspirations, beliefs, convictions, and attractions. Even aversions and fears may indicate something about potential value formation if I take time for reflection and identify the steps I have not yet taken.

The Dynamics of Conversion

Think back to the first section of this chapter, where the emphasis was on *reflection* as an important step in the learning process. To say that reflection is thinking about something that we experience or learn does not explain precisely how we reflect. Bernard Lonergan has given us a method for understanding the *what* and *how* of the learning process. The method is a dynamic series of operations, each building on the other.[2]

If we observe what we do in coming to an insight about something, we discover that we are following interior commands or imperatives that arise without our bidding when we do not interfere in the process. In point of fact there are many kinds of interferences that create biases in our learning; nevertheless, it is very useful to grasp the method in its pure form.

The first imperative is, "Be attentive," or "Pay attention." When we pay attention to something carefully, we are led to ask such questions as, "What is it? What is it for?" Ordinarily we are very certain when we don't understand something. We say, "I don't get it," or, "It is beyond me." When we have the experience of understanding something, we say, "I get it," or, "Now I see," or, "I understand."

So far we have considered the experience of two commands: "Be attentive," and "Be understanding." These are called "transcendental imperatives or commands," because through them we reach beyond ourselves. Once we understand, other questions arise, and we experience another command: "Be reasonable." To be reasonable we check out our understanding; we compare it with other related understandings to see if there are important data or perspectives that we may have missed.

At this point an example may be useful. Consider John, who pays attention to Sally at work, begins to date her, and falls in love with her. His entire view of life undergoes a dramatic change. He now understands love with an immediacy that no written words by the most gifted poet could ever have provided him. He wants to spend the rest of his life with Sally. Here a new imperative arises: "Be reasonable." There are many things to consider before he can responsibly propose marriage. He carefully reflects on the consequences of marriage, on his own capabilities and limitations, and also on Sally's as far as he knows them. He reasonably spends time with Sally so that they can come to know each other better. If he reasonably concludes that marriage is a good course of action, he experiences another internal imperative: "Be responsible," which in this case may mean that he will ask Sally to marry him. If she says "Yes," the example presumes that Sally has also been attentive, understanding, and reasonable, and has come to the same conclusion as John.

All this may seem obvious once we trace the sequence of operations: Be attentive, be understanding, be reasonable, be responsible. In practice, very often we probably do not follow this sequence of operations perfectly. Contributing to a less than perfect performance may be our biases, prejudices, laziness, fatigue, habits, and also social pressures of various kinds. If we keep trying, however, we will not only improve our chances of coming to a good conclusion, whatever the matter at hand, but we will change ourselves for the better in the process. This will be the case whether we are trying to figure out a possible course of action, master a body of knowledge, make an important decision, or even if we are writing an article or preparing a speech. In the process we will have undergone several conversions: an intellectual conversion in being attentive, understanding, and reasonable, and a moral conversion in being responsible. It may help to think of the transcendental imperatives as *calls,* as *vocation,* rather than as commands.

If there is a call, there has to be a caller, and this raises the question of the caller's identity. What, or who, calls us to be attentive, understanding, reasonable, and responsible, that is, to develop our human potential, to become mature with an inner freedom that makes us at one and the same time respondents to a caller and self-directed persons? To the question, "What calls us to respond?" the answer is conscience. This is true in small things—"Shall I eat this cake?"—and in major decisions—"Shall I marry Sally?" "Shall I take this executive position offered by a company that employs sweatshop labor overseas?" Justice and injustice, peace and violence in the social arena, as well as personal short-comings, are the consequence of not heeding the transcendental imperatives. On the personal level, we may be living a kind of stimulus-response existence, adjusting to pressures from within and without, possibly even leading lives of quiet desperation.

If our question is not "What calls?" but "Who calls?" we give the ultimate caller a name. Our name for the caller is God. At this point the conversion process has moved to religious conversion, that is, to a response to one who invites us to transcendence, who calls us to a recognition of the deepest understanding of all, namely, that we are called by name by one who loves us. When we are grasped by that experience we are changed forever. The best adventure of our lives can be the experience of falling in love and being in love with God. It changes everything: what we want to pay attention to, and how we pay attention, what we understand about anything, what is reasonable and what being responsible asks of us. Obeying the transcendental imperatives will still require work, but it will be a work of love in an atmosphere of deep inner joy and peace. Love, joy, and peace are the first fruits of the Holy Spirit (Gal 5:22), and they are always found together. This is true even in situations of sorrow and pain.

Lonergan writes:

> Religious conversion goes beyond moral. Questions for intelligence, for reflection, for deliberation reveal the eros of the human spirit, its capacity and its desire for self-transcendence. But that capacity meets fulfillment, that desire turns into joy, when religious conversion transforms the existential subject into a subject in love, a subject held, grasped, possessed, owned through a total and so an other-worldly love. Then there is a new basis for all valuing and all doing good. In no way are fruits of intellectual or moral conversion negated or diminished. On the contrary, all human pursuit of the true and the good is included

within and furthered by a cosmic context and purpose and, as well, there now accrues to man the power of love to enable him to accept the suffering involved in undoing the effects of decline.[3]

In explaining religious conversion, Lonergan often quotes a passage from Saint Paul's Letter to the Romans 5:5: " God's love has been poured into our hearts through the Holy Spirit that has been given to us." The work of religious conversion that forever changes our perspective and our motivation is God's initiative. We do not earn the love of God. God loves us, each of us personally and all of us together, infinitely, out of sheer goodness and divine freedom. To the extent that we are grasped by this experience, our effort to work for justice and peace is no longer experienced as a project in which God is helping us. Rather, we come to understand ourselves as privileged to participate as lovers in God's own ongoing work in the world. The important question becomes not one of success but one of fidelity. How all this can work out in practice is the subject matter for the remainder of this book.

QUESTIONS AND EXERCISES FOR STUDY, REFLECTION, AND CONVERSATION

1. Explain the difference between subjective and objective values. Why is this distinction important?
2. Discuss social and economic values that contribute to the good of society, and those that contribute to injustice and violence.
3. Identify some of your value indicators and note how you can use them to develop genuine values. Be specific.
4. The following exercise is to be done with another person or in a small group. Here are seven things that many people value or aspire to value. Mark the one you value most highly as 1, and the one you value least as 7.

Keeping my word   ——

Taking care of my health   ——

Finding satisfaction in my work   ——

Living in a society in which human rights are highly respected   ——

Economic justice for all people   ——

Living in a secure society   ——

Other (be specific) ____

Next, tell each other why you ranked an item as first or seventh. The sharing of reasons for your choices will help clarify your values and value indicators.

5. This exercise is to be done privately. Make a time chart for a week, keeping track of how much time you spend in various activities, including everything you do in your free time. Then ask yourself (a) How do I feel about the way I spent my time? How do I judge the way I spent my time? (b) What proportion of my time was spent in activities that express my deepest values? (c) What inconsistencies, if any, were there in the week's activities? Repeat this exercise every few months. Keep track of the answers. How we spend time reveals much about our values. This exercise can be repeated, substituting money for time.

6. Reflect on specific personal experiences in which being attentive led to your being understanding, reasonable, and responsible. See if you can identify obstacles to the sequence of these operations. How did you handle them?

7. Discuss Bernard Lonergan's explanation of religious conversion as "being in love."

8. Does the section on the Dynamics of Conversion in this chapter help you to a deeper understanding of work for justice and peace?

NOTES

1. For a process of personally clarifying one's values, I am indebted to Louis E. Raths, Merrill Harmin, and Sidney B. Simon, *Values and Teaching* (Columbus, OH: Charles E. Merrill, 1966), although I do not agree with the authors' definition of value.

2. Bernard J. F. Lonergan, *Method in Theology* (Toronto: University of Toronto Press, 1994). See also many useful articles in Vernon Gregson, ed., *The Desires of the Human Heart: An Introduction to the Theology of Bernard Lonergan* (New York/Mahwah, NJ: Paulist Press, 1988).

3. Lonergan, *Method in Theology*, 242.

CHAPTER SEVEN

— ✢ —

Knowing Where We Live

When Jesus turned and saw them following, he said to them,
"What are you looking for?" They said to him, "Rabbi"
(which translated means Teacher), "where are you staying?"
He said to them, "Come and see."
—John 1:38–39

CHAPTER FOCUS

We live simultaneously in a number of contexts or "spaces": intrapersonal, interpersonal, societal, and ecological. While we can define these clearly, and each has its own possibilities and demands, our actions in all these areas impact each other. We have responsibilities in each of these dimensions of our lives. Dealing with the societal dimension requires that we understand the constitutive parts of social institutions. The newest challenge we face is coming to terms with human responsibility for the ecological dimension of our lives.

Where We Live

If someone asks me where I live, my answer depends not only on where I am, but also where my questioner is. If I am in Sweden and someone asks me, "Where do you live?" I first answer that I live in the United States. However, if I happen to be in New York, I answer, "Cincinnati," the city I call home. If someone in Cincinnati asks me where I live, I answer with my street address. Where we live is always relative to some other place. Seen from another point of view, we live in several places at once. We can represent this by concentric circles.

Intrapersonal Space

Intrapersonal space refers to what is going on inside us. In fact, much of our living is contained within us in our intrapersonal space. A person may have a rich life without moving from a room or even from a chair. This intrapersonal life is represented by the innermost circle in Figure 2.

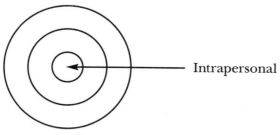

Intrapersonal

FIGURE 2

How I live this intrapersonal life makes all the difference when I do rise from my chair and leave my room. Whether I am in Sweden or New York or at home in Cincinnati, I am selfish or generous, reflective or shallow, kindly disposed or seething with anger and envy. The possibilities are many, and I cannot avoid them. From the moral perspective, there is no neutral intrapersonal life; the possibilities for deeper development of all that is best in me continue throughout my life.

The quality of the intrapersonal dimension of our lives is crucial in work for social justice, reconciliation, and peace building. How we learn, and how we clarify and develop our values are two important dimensions of intrapersonal life already discussed in chapters 5 and 6. There are other related dimensions. For example, to the extent that we are at peace within ourselves, we have the inner freedom to be attentive to what is outside us and the inner resources to deal with the external reality, whatever it is. This is something to keep in mind as we, along with others, ponder the possibilities of helping to build justice into our social structures and of preventing violence and healing the wounds, physical and emotional, that violence inflicts. When a certain soldier accosted a Buddhist monk with the words, "Do you realize that I can run you through with this sword without batting an eye?" the monk replied, "Do you realize that I can let you run me through with that sword without batting an eye?" The monk's reply under pressure reveals the quality of his intrapersonal life.

We can develop a kind of inner radar or early warning system to deal with violence and injustice in propaganda, in abusive language, in economic discrimination, in stereotyping, and in denial and suppression of people's needs and rights. If our own intrapersonal life is not healthy, we may find it difficult or even impossible to see these issues and to deal with them constructively. To be in touch with one's own intrapersonal life is not an automatic process. For this reason, time set aside for reflection, meditation, and prayer as well as for rest and recreation is not time taken from work for justice and peace; rather, it is an integral part of that work and one oñ which all the rest depends.

The quality of life demonstrated by some famous prisoners of conscience demonstrates well the potential strength and splendor of the intrapersonal life. Take the case of Nelson Mandela. After twenty-seven years in prison, where he was deprived of normal social interaction and subjected to harsh and demeaning conditions, he emerged from prison a more splendid person than when he began his long incarceration. Also, Martin Luther King Jr.'s "Letter from a Birmingham Jail" and Gandhi's autobiography *The Story of My Experiments with Truth* each reveal a person who entered prison with a rich intrapersonal life, developed it further in most difficult conditions, and even while in prison produced works that still nourish the human spirit.

Interpersonal Space

We spend a major part of our lives and a great deal of energy interacting with others: family members, colleagues, neighbors, relatives, and friends, and with many other people with whom we associate in our normal activity, from the person who checks us out at the supermarket to the doctor, the pastor, the elderly neighbor we take to the super market. This is the interpersonal dimension of our lives (represented in Figure 3 by the middle circle). We are radically social by nature, and without others our lives would have come to an end very quickly. We experience the greatest joy in life, or its absence, in relationship to others.

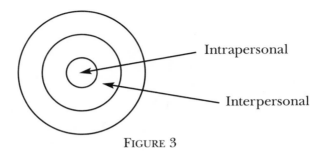

The way we live on the interpersonal level has a great impact on any efforts for a more just and peaceful world. We reach the political through the interpersonal. People who are passionate about social justice and peace may be very good at writing protest letters, but they may not be very adept in writing letters that express sincere appreciation for what a public figure has done well or that recognize the difficulty of dealing with a particular political issue. However, we can grow in the capacity to write in a way that is both supportive and challenging, as the following story illustrates.

A friend told me that she received a personal phone call from a U.S. Congressman one Sunday evening. He called to thank her for a short letter she had written, thanking and commending him for his courage during a television interview in which he took a position against the bombing of Belgrade during the war in Kosovo. She had also commented appreciatively on the way he defended his position on both moral and political grounds. Her letter and his return phone call paved the way for a continuing contact on other political issues.

I once joined two other members of my community to visit three state representatives when they were home in their districts. One member of our group worked with women who were just getting off welfare and learning to manage a budget. The women's success in making this transition depended in part on stability in utility rates that were capped at a certain level for people in their circumstances. We were lobbying for legislation that would keep the cap on the utility rates, and we were equipped with facts and with the direct experience of one member of our group. In this particular effort we were successful, but even had the issue gone the other way we had begun relationships that we could build on in other advocacy efforts.

It is important to develop good interpersonal relationships within peace and justice movements and organizations themselves, including social justice committees in neighborhoods and parishes. The number of those investing time and training in working for social change is relatively small. There are many reasons for this, including the fact that many good people are put off by the manner of some justice and peace advocates. Society needs many more people who will act as advocates for those whose rights are not honored and whose needs are not met. Skill in interpersonal relations can play a major role in enlarging the number of those who are effectively working on the side of the poor for a more just and peaceful society.

Some virtues are especially appropriate in the interpersonal arena of our lives. How to cultivate them is not within the scope of this book, but it is useful to know a few places where these interpersonal virtues are identified. For example, the Letter of Saint Paul to the Galatians confronts a situation of serious conflict in the community. Some insisted that Christians must observe all the Jewish laws and customs; others did not consider themselves bound by these obligations. Paul was very clearly on the side of the latter. The issue was central to his teaching. He wrote, "You are separated from Christ, you who are trying to be justified by law; you have fallen from grace. For through the Spirit, by faith, we await the hope of righteousness. For in Christ Jesus, neither circumcision nor uncircumcision counts for anything, but only faith working through love" (Gal 5:4–6). He went on to enumerate the fruits of the Spirit, in effect, a short list of the qualities needed to restore good relationship in a divided community. "The fruit of the spirit is love, joy, peace, patience, kindness, generosity, faithfulness, gentleness, self-control" (Gal 5:22). While this list of the qualities needed in good interpersonal relationships is not complete, even a brief reflection on these nine qualities suffices to emphasize that how we pursue our cause is just as important for winning a hearing as being on the right side of an issue.

Societal Space

There are probably times when we would like to confine our activities to the intrapersonal and interpersonal dimensions of our lives; after all, in both contexts there is more to do than we can adequately accomplish. However, there is another context, the societal dimension (the outermost circle in Figure 4), which also makes its claims on us. In this context, activity is organized to achieve social, economic, and political objectives that go beyond interpersonal possibilities.

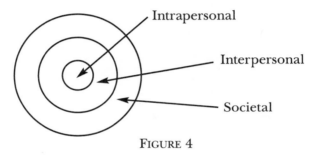

FIGURE 4

In the societal dimension we find job descriptions; here persons have roles to play that are more or less clearly defined within established social structures or social institutions and systems. We accept the benefits of those who provide basic services we cannot provide for ourselves, including such necessities as sanitation, safe water and food, health care and education, and transportation that stretches beyond our local and national boundaries. It is a basic injustice to accept these benefits of the societal dimension without bearing reciprocal responsibilities for the quality of life of society.

Throughout history, millions of men and women have lived under the rule of absolute monarchs, or in totalitarian regimes dependent on a few persons who made all the critical decisions about their subjects' lives in the societal context and often invaded their private lives as well. The long ages of such political arrangements are over in principle, or so we hope. Today people all over the world aspire to constitutional government, that is, government by law rather than by arbitrary personal power. However, the gap between the ideal and the actual is great. Participatory democracy does not work of itself; it is worked by the people. This calls for particular commitments and abilities beyond those required in the intrapersonal and interpersonal contexts of people's lives. A most serious defect in the societal context is not only the occasional emergence of a ruthless dictator, but also the apathy of people who accept the benefits in the societal context without assuming the responsibilities of citizenship, who opt out of their responsibilities in society. Who of us is willing to forego societal benefits? In a world now inhabited by more than six billion people, we share responsibility for the global common good.

In our day we have seen the multiplication of thousands of nongovernmental organizations, or NGOs, working on issues of the societal dimension of life, issues that go beyond interpersonal relations. NGOs do not comprise all of civil society, but they are a very significant part of it, and their growth is evidence of the goodness and resilience of the human spirit that continues to reach for ever fuller exercise of our human potential. Within every country, in some more than others, this growth in organizations of civil society needs more support in order to develop better ways of communicating and networking. One index of the quality of life of a society is the range and effectiveness of its nongovernmental organizations that together contribute so much to the quality of life.[1]

Besides this kind of organizational development, there are cultural developments that influence many facets of society. On the international level, for example, the United Nations Economic, Scientific, and Cultural Organization (UNESCO) has launched a program called "A Culture of Peace and Nonviolence," which aims to help ensure that the conflicts inherent in human relationships are resolved nonviolently. Programs in this international effort include the training of parliamentarians and elected officials in the fundamentals of good governance, democracy and social justice, the empowerment of women to enable them to participate effectively in postwar reconciliation processes, and retraining and social reinsertion of demobilized soldiers. Other related civic education programs address such needs as training in leadership and in conflict management. UNESCO's Culture of Peace and Nonviolence program demonstrates that there is a large area of life where the line between the interpersonal and societal dimensions of life is not always perfectly clear. At the same time, the distinction between the various dimensions of our lives is very useful, helping us understand the many possibilities for working constructively for social change and enabling us to have clear objectives for our actions.[2]

Anatomy of Institutions

Effective work for social justice and peace requires more than a general notion that social institutions need to be changed; we also need to know the "anatomy" of institutions. Anatomy is the art of separating the parts of an animal or plant in order to ascertain their position, relations, structure, and function. Analogous to the anatomy of plants or animals is the anatomy of institutions. An institution—the word comes from a Latin verb that means "to stand"—is a social body, an established and stable way of doing something significant in society. In a very real sense an institution stands there, giving society some degree of stability and order so that people can get on with matters that concern them. Institutions are predictable. It is good that some things are predictable when we wake up in the morning; otherwise we might never have the courage to get out of bed.

The related term *structure* is used frequently as a synonym for *institution;* sometimes it refers to a complex set of institutions. The same is true of *system* when used in the present context. We speak of political systems and economic systems in this way. For our purposes here, once we have a grasp of the constituent parts of an institution we can apply this knowledge to complex structures and systems. An institution is a human creation, something that is constructed, not something that we find or that happens. Often an institution or a system needs to be changed because it is not working well or does not serve the purpose for which it was created. To attempt institutional change without a clear understanding of what makes up an institution would be like trying to become a doctor without studying anatomy. Let us now consider the eight parts of that anatomy.

Eight Constitutive Parts
of a Social Institution

Every social institution, from the Girl Scouts to the United Nations, has eight constitutive parts. The importance of this will become increasingly clear as we take up the issue of social change further on in this chapter.

First, every social institution has a *body of beliefs, values, and practices* that are generally accepted by the members and also by those who are not a part of the institution but who interact with it in some way. Consider the example of so simple but important an institution as a fire department in a community. If both the personnel and the citizens did not have a common understanding or belief about what is expected of a fire department, the department would be a dysfunctional and useless institution. In an emergency we could call and find no one in, or discover that the department had decided not to provide services to those who had not voted in the past two elections.

Sometimes, but not necessarily, the basic beliefs, values, and practices of an institution are written in a basic descriptive document, a constitution. The actual constitution is not the document; the constitution is, rather, the way the parts work together, and that depends on the condition of each part. When we say that a person has a strong physical constitution, we mean precisely how well the entire organism functions, all its various organs and systems doing what they are meant to do for the good of the whole body. Analogously, when a society works well, it has a strong constitution, whether or not it has a written document that describes the constitution. Today almost all states see to it that they have a written constitution, a document that serves as a reference for making laws and for judging whether something is in violation of a basic constitutional principle, a basic belief, or value of the society.

Second, every institution has some *laws* or at least some *regulations* that clarify the rights and responsibilities of those who make up the institution. In a family, the most fundamental institution of every society, if there is not some kind of unwritten law regarding the relationship of parents to each other, of parents to children, and of children to parents and to each other, the family will not hold together well. This shows that in small familiar institutions law is not thought of as law and need not be written, and probably should not be written. However, without an established set of requirements flowing from shared values, the group may constantly be trying to settle problems, using in this way a great deal of energy that could be used more effectively and enjoyably in other ways.

A family and other small groups can get along without written regulations. Society, on the other hand, does have written laws regarding the expected behavior of parents toward children. For example, parents may not abuse their children, and they must ensure that their children will receive a basic education. Governments make laws regarding child abuse because it is not a private matter in a society that has a respect for human rights. These rights are inherent in the person prior to one's position in the family. Governments also make laws concerning education because education involves public as well as personal rights and responsibilities. The relationship between parents' and society's rights and responsibilities for the education of children requires constant vigilance.

Third, an institution has some *material goods, its property, that belong to the institution.* How the property belongs, whether it is rented, held in trust, or with some title to ownership, is a legal matter. The family needs a house, the fire department needs a place for personnel and equipment, the students and teachers need a place for learning and teaching, and so on. Sometimes a building is actually equated with an institution, and though this is not what is meant by *institution* in the present context, the fact that the word is used also to refer to buildings suggests that ordinarily property of some kind is integral to a social institution. A great many challenges and problems arise when an institution's property does not match the institution's needs or its beliefs and values.

Fourth, an institution needs a *way of indoctrination,* of handing on in its totality the institution's beliefs, values, practices, laws, and regulations. If it does not have an effective way of doing this, it will not be able to attract or keep new members or participants. For example, educational institutions have catalogs, mission statements, and faculty and student handbooks and orientation programs. Nations have flags, holidays, parades, and required courses in schools. Today many institutions write mission statements to express publicly their beliefs and values and ways they intend to implement them.

For many people, the word *indoctrination* has negative over-tones suggesting propaganda, manipulative methods, and oppressive and totalitarian regimes. While indoctrination can be evil, a violation of personal freedom, this is not necessarily the case. Every institution needs some ways of succinctly explaining itself to its new and prospective members and to those who, while not members, will want to work with the institution. Failure to indoctrinate in the positive sense of the term puts too great a burden of discovery on the new and prospective members and associates.

Fifth, an institution needs a *way of keeping regular contact* with those who make up the institution or relate to it on a regular basis. This essential component is *communication* and is not the same as indoctrination, which deals with the fundamental makeup of the institution. Communication keeps people in touch with each other and with the institution's activities and changes and nurtures their sense of belonging. Communication is important to large complex institutions, such as a large hospital that has a whole array of communication devices. Perhaps more than any other constitutive part of an institution, communication brings home to us that it is people who make up every institution, and that the quality of their lives depends essentially on the quality of their relationships, on how they communicate. A strong case can be made that the single most telling indicator of the quality of life of any institution is the quality of the communication among those who are part of it or who relate to it in some significant way. If communication is open, respectful, truthful, sensitive to the needs and best aspirations of all, if it is kind and compassionate to those suffering or vulnerable, if it helps people know and appreciate their rights and responsibilities and tells them where to give and receive assistance and service, chances are that the institution is very healthy.

The sixth constitutive element of every institution is its *economy*. The economy is the institution's systematic way of managing its resources in light of its values and purpose. An institution may be materially poor, but with a good economy it may move toward its goals in an effective way. On the other hand, an institution without a sound economy is in for trouble. The greatest asset of any institution is not money, but people who know clearly what the goals of the enterprise are and have a good plan for moving toward those goals. An institution that begins with few material resources can be effective if it has a strong sense of mission, a solidly thought out economy or management plan, and good communication with its members and others it wants to serve.

The seventh part of an institution is its *government*. The form of government varies from one institution to another. Simple institutions that exist in great numbers in every society may need very little formal government, but they cannot get along without some—an institution without a government would be like a rowing team without a captain. It is important to have clarity about governmental authority: what kind, who has it, and how far the authority extends. This is true not only of political institutions, but also of schools, corporations, churches, and all other social institutions. Within the past two hundred years, constitutional democracies have become the normative form for governments, and all indicators are that the trend will continue, though not without resistance and the ever-present problem of citizen apathy.

People tend to be wary about government, and with reason. Government and power to control go hand in hand. Power brings with it the temptation to abuse it in one's own favor. Domination entails submission. Political power, however, moves along a continuum from dominance/submission at one end to a high level of participation and mutuality at the other. Good government is not static; it is always moving in one direction or the other on that continuum.

An eighth part is crucial to keep an institution viable. Every institution needs some *method of evaluation, renewal, and at times reform*. Though institutional self-examination is not easy and often avoided, the price of avoidance is high. Life is not static. All around, other institutions are beginning, changing, and in some cases going out of existence. Unless an institution adjusts to what is happening around it, it may find itself in a cultural vacuum, out of touch with the larger society it started out to serve. This does not mean that those directing an institution should trim its sails to every wind that blows. It may be that in a renewal effort those responsible for the institution will conclude that it needs to take a direction different from the mainstream. Failure to engage in the effort of evaluation and renewal can mean the decline and even the demise of a social institution that had been doing good work and holding great promise but that neglected regular review and evaluation.

Every institution possesses these eight components. We will look at them again in chapter 9, in considering social analysis and imagination as important in work for social justice and peace. First, however, we turn to one more dimension in which we live.

Ecological Space

Besides the intrapersonal, the interpersonal, and the societal dimensions, there is yet one more space we inhabit. Like the air we breathe, we ordinarily take this other space for granted unless something signals that we are in trouble. Ecological space refers to the entire planetary system that is the physical context of our lives. Another circle added to the set of concentric circles that we've been developing would distort rather than clarify the notion of ecological space. It is not beyond the other contexts of our lives. Think instead that the shading in Figure 5 represents the fact that all the contexts of our lives are part of our ecological space.

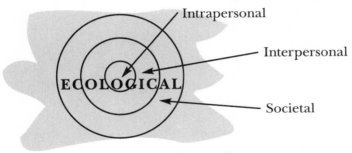

FIGURE 5

Until the 1970s in the United States and in some other highly industrialized societies, a prevalent myth was that we live on a self-renewing planet with unlimited resources, so that we could take all we wanted from the earth and do anything to the earth that we judged to be in our own narrow interests. We did not see the need to concern ourselves much with the long-range consequences. There were always some people who knew better, but their specialized knowledge was not part of the conventional wisdom.

Those days are gone forever. As a human race we are now struggling to shape a vision that must inform public policies and foster the political will to care for the planet, including its atmosphere, so that it can continue to serve as the dwelling place for a myriad of forms of life. We are in a crisis in the strict sense, at a turning point that is unavoidable. Unlike some other crises in the intrapersonal, interpersonal, and societal dimensions of life, this one requires widespread understanding of some of the complexities of our physical interdependence and calls for a profound intellectual, moral, and religious conversion, from seeing the earth as belonging to us, to seeing that we belong to the earth.

QUESTIONS FOR STUDY, REFLECTION, AND CONVERSATION

1. Reflect on the feelings you experience when you are in touch with your intrapersonal life. What do you do when you do not have inner peace?

2. This chapter cites persons who grew in character under extremely difficult circumstances. What can we learn from them?

3. Compose a letter to a legislator about an issue he or she may have to deal with. Discuss the letter with another person, or discuss it with a group. Send the letter.

4. Reflect on the fruits of the Spirit in Galatians 5:22 (p. 89). Do you see these as qualities of good interpersonal relations? Would you add others? Does this exercise help you identify particular fruits that you want to cultivate in your life?

5. Discuss ways to promote "A Culture of Peace and Nonviolence" (p. 91).

6. Identify, as far as you can, the beliefs, values, and practices of your local fire department or some other local public institution. You may want to conduct an interview with some of the personnel.

7. Choose an institution with which you are very familiar. Identify its eight constitutive parts. Do you see ways that any of the parts can be improved? Where would you start? Why? (Note: Ways of working for social change are taken up in the next chapters.)

8. Discuss ways in which awareness of ecological space is influencing: (a) your personal life, (b) society, (c) career choices, (d) justice and peace movements.

NOTES

1. See "Crafting Civic Culture through International Nongovernmental Organizations," in Elise Boulding, *Building a Global Civic Culture: Education for an Interdependent World* (Syracuse, NY: Syracuse University Press, 1988), 118–39; and Jackie Smith, Charles Chatfield, and Ron Pagnucco, eds., *Transnational Social Movements and Global Politics: Solidarity beyond the State* (Syracuse, NY: Syracuse University Press, 1997).

2. See the UNESCO Web site: http://www3.unesco.org/iycp/ (click on *Peace Is in Our Hands* on the Culture of Peace home page). See also the message of Pope John Paul II for the World Day of Peace 2001, "Dialogue between Cultures for a Civilization of Love and Peace," Origins 30(29), January 4, 2001, 458–64.

CHAPTER EIGHT

— ❖ —

The Impact of Culture

And for all this, nature is never spent;
  There lives the dearest freshness deep down things;
And though the last lights off the black West went
  Oh, morning, at the brown brink eastward, springs–
Because the Holy Ghost over the bent
  World broods with warm breast and with ah! bright wings.
  —Gerard Manley Hopkins, SJ, "God's Grandeur"

CHAPTER FOCUS

Profound cultural shifts affect our work for social change. Four of the major shifts are in the areas of ecology, feminist consciousness, changes in the place of war, and new insight into the primacy of love, understood as solidarity. Essential for social change are a sense of timing and an understanding of the ways both grace and sin are embedded in culture and institutions.

Belonging to the Earth

The need to belong is a most basic human need. Our sense of where we belong determines how we find our security and our sense of identity. Generally speaking, we feel we belong first of all to a particular family and to the country in which we live rather than to the Earth. Although in some ways this is true, the problem is that we tend to identify so strongly with our political community, our nation, that we may not realize that our first identification is with the Earth, not with our particular country or even with the human race. This identification with the Earth binds us more closely to each other than we may ever have imagined. Science today can help us enlarge our vision, change our point of view. According to David Toolan:

> Every moment, a portion of the body's trillions of atoms is dissipating to the world outside, and 98 percent of them are replaced annually. Each time we breathe, we take in a quadrillion atoms breathed by the rest of humanity within the last two weeks, and more than a million breathed personally sometime by each and any person on earth. So much for the strictly bounded, separate individual.[1]

Along with the recognition that nothing is static is the growing awareness that our planet Earth and its resources are limited and also out of balance. The Earth is not a limitless depository of raw materials for human consumption; it is a delicate system of which we humans are a part. This fact calls us to move from a stance of exploitation of nature to one of benign presence to nature.[2]

Today there is a growing sense that we belong to the Earth before we belong to any other group or community, whether family, church, or nation. It is here that we must make our fundamental commitments as human beings. In the words of Brian Swimme, the central insight of our era must be "that the universe is a communion of subjects rather than a collection of objects."[3] To say that the universe is a communion of subjects is to acknowledge our intricate interdependence as actors, down to the smallest particles. Everything is acting on everything else, and at the smallest discernible level of material creation it is not possible to tell where matter and energy begin and end in their interdependence.

Women Coming into Their Own

Women's movements both reflect and propel another basic cultural shift we are now experiencing. It is incontrovertible that women and men are equal in fundamental human dignity, the basis of human rights. We have paid lip service to this truth and believed it as a proposition, but in practice women have been treated as subordinate to men. That is now changing in a way unprecedented in history. Sandra Schneiders writes, "As the human enterprise gradually comes to be seen as a two-sex experience, values such as recognition of the other, equality, mutuality, relationality, interdependence, and cooperation are beginning to appear as not only 'women's strange ways of being' but as a human way of being that may be preferable to imperialism, domination, rugged individualism, and competition."[4]

Terrorism Challenges the Ways of War

September 11, 2001, marks the beginning of a third signifi-cant cultural shift in our sense of belonging. Here the accent is on how belonging is related to the fundamental need for security. The terrorist attacks against the United States mark a watershed in the way states have customarily provided for the security of their populations against outside aggression. Terrorism has now demonstrated that military might cannot provide security for a nation; rather, security depends on good will that is the fruit of justice. War may continue within states and smaller groups, but interstate warfare as planned and carried out by the highly indus-trialized states has been outsmarted by the ingenuity of relatively poor people, though with considerable financial resources from some who are not poor.

This situation may well lead to a more widespread search for alternatives to violence, to increased efforts to bring active nonvi-olence into institutional efforts at peacemaking. People promot-ing alternatives to violence are already found in peace movements as well as in educational institutions, diplomatic circles, and even within the military, as a significant though minor voice. Throughout this book I argue that the potential of love raised to the political level is more powerful than any weaponry. Today there is a fresh cultural opportunity to demonstrate that truth, and an urgency to do so. We risk failure just as we have always risked failure in war. But we are also implicitly called to heroism, even to the giving of our life in efforts to deal with violence by rejecting ways of killing of the enemy in favor of ways of over-coming the enmity. We may be learning the truth of the words of Martin Luther King Jr.: "The ultimate weakness of violence is that it is a descending spiral, begetting the very thing it seeks to destroy....Returning violence for violence multiplies violence, adding deeper darkness to a night already devoid of stars.

Darkness cannot drive out darkness; only light can do that. Hate cannot drive out hate; only love can do that."[5]

Love Expressed as Solidarity

A fourth cultural shift in which we participate is within our understanding of Christian faith and practice. More than ever we can now see how essential it is for Christians to ground their action for justice and peace in a lived relationship with Jesus Christ in a community of disciples. Jesus' words in John's Gospel—"I am the way, and the truth, and the life (John 14:6)—have meaning for society, not only for individuals. Jesus taught us how to live and die, not how to kill. We can expect to see active nonviolence move more rapidly from the periphery to the center of Christian moral vision and theology. Rational convictions about the bankruptcy of various forms of violence will not produce an alternative to violence. Only experiments with love and truth will do that. We can expect to see more clearly the intrinsic relationship between specific issues of justice and issues of peace.

The terrorist actions of September 11, 2001, will be seen more and more as a wake-up call. Nothing can justify the actions that killed thousands of persons, but an understanding of justice and injustice can help us understand the significance of the event and help us draw lessons from it. Few who read this book will have experienced the despair-inducing poverty and subjection of the world's wretchedly poor people. Poverty as it exists in the world today is rooted in greed and selfishness endemic in political, economic, and social structures. The wealthiest corporations that are driven by growth as a goal have much more political power than most states, and they have not been held accountable for the consequences of their policies. This reinforces the belief that limitless acquisition is morally acceptable. The consequence is a growing gap between the rich and the poor.

Solidarity is a term used in Pope John Paul II's social teaching, and consistently developed by him, to describe the love that unites personal and societal action:

It is above all a question of interdependence, sensed as a system determining relationships in the contemporary

world, in its economic, cultural, political, and religious elements, and accepted as a moral category. When interdependence becomes recognized in this way, the correlative
response as a moral and social attitude, as a "virtue," is solidarity. This then is not a feeling of vague compassion or
shallow distress at the misfortunes of so many people, both
near and far. On the contrary, it is a firm and persevering
determination to commit oneself to the common good;
that is to say to the good of all and of each individual,
because we are all really responsible for all....

The exercise of solidarity within each society is valid
when its members recognize one another as
persons....Solidarity helps us to see the "other"—whether a
person, people, or nation—not just as some kind of instru-
ment, with a work capacity and physical strength to be
exploited at low cost and then discarded when no longer
useful, but as our "neighbor," a "helper" (cf. Gen 2:18–20),
to be made a sharer, on a par with ourselves, in the banquet of life to which all are equally invited by God. Hence
the importance of reawakening the religious awareness of
individuals and peoples.[6]

Pope John Paul links solidarity closely with the culture of peace:

The culture of solidarity is closely connected with the
value of peace, the primary objective of every society and
of national and international life. However, on the path
to better understanding among peoples there remain
many challenges which the world must face. These set
before everyone choices which cannot be postponed. The
alarming increase of arms, together with the halting
progress of commitment to nuclear nonproliferation,
runs the risk of feeding and expanding a culture of competition and conflict, a culture involving not only states
but also non-institutional entities such as paramilitary
groups and terrorist organizations.

Even today the world is dealing with the consequences
of wars past and present as well as the tragic effects of anti-
personnel mines and the use of frightful chemical and biological weapons. And what can be said about the
permanent risk of conflicts between nations, of civil wars
within some states, and of widespread violence, before

which international organizations and national governments appear almost impotent? Faced with such threats,
everyone must feel the moral duty to take concrete and
timely steps to promote the cause of peace and understanding among peoples.[7]

Structures of Grace and Structures of Sin

It is essential that we understand how these cultural shifts
are related to the meaning and purpose of our lives. One way to
begin is to consider the development of the notions of structures
of grace and structures of sin. The basic meaning of grace is gift,
and the fundamental gift of God to us is a share in God's own life.
In a broad sense, all gifts of God that enable us to live according
to our meaning and destiny are graces. To understand this is an
intellectual conversion. As noted moral theologian Richard
McCormick, SJ, wrote:

> We must see our moral life from the inside out. When we
> see it this way, we see it not above all as fragmented acts
> responding to do's and don'ts; we see it not primarily as
> successes and failure, but as a precious gift entrusted to
> us—the friendship of God in His Son and through His
> Spirit. Like any friendship, this one must be nourished and
> fostered with mutual conversation, exchange of gifts,
> moments of quiet, strenuous acts of protection and resist-
> ance and glorious celebrations.
>
> When we see our moral spiritual life in this way, we see
> it as a growth process, a gradual unfolding or drying up of
> our personal beings as Christians. This is what the Holy
> Spirit is operating within us. It is this life that we try to
> deepen with reflection on God's word, with nourishment
> in the Eucharist. It is the life that we try to protect and fos-
> ter with constant but joyful conversion of heart in the
> sacrament of reconciliation. It is this life that we try to
> express in caring for the needs of others and in protecting
> their rights.
>
> In this notion of our lives-in-Christ, freedom in its most
> fundamental sense is not a given quantity, but a task to be
> achieved through a lifetime. It is an acorn to be nourished

into the oak. In cooperation with the Holy Spirit we extend our freedom, our liberation; we tighten our cling upon our God. That is the very meaning of constant conversion of heart; for even though we are converted in heart, we are not totally so.[8]

Notice that McCormick says that we express our graced lives "in caring for the needs of others and in protecting their rights." When we do this we act through institutions in order to be effective, and so we can accurately say that grace inheres in these institutions, in their values, regulations, budgets, governance, ways of communicating, in all the eight components of social institutions identified in chapter 7. Graced social structures multiply our effectiveness in expressing love of God and neighbor, and in some cases actually make the expression of that love possible.

The following example makes this clear. In December 2000 three men in their thirties who had been in prison for fifteen years were released after the charges filed against them were dismissed. A caring and competent lawyer who defended them was able to win the case on the basis of evidence from DNA. Without legal and scientific institutions, the men might have spent their entire lives in prison. There are very probably others in prison who should not be there. Compassion and commitment to justice alone will not win their release; only compassion and justice working within and through social structures can do that.

Graced institutions are as diverse as the birthday cake, which is a cultural institution; the Eucharist, which is a sacramental institution; and Alcoholics Anonymous and hospice care, which are two social institutions of relatively recent invention. While these institutions depend on the quality of service of each person who contributes to them, as institutions they embody grace in ways that are patterned and stable, that can be counted on, that can express love in effective ways beyond the capacity of a single person to show love to someone, or to care for a person's or group's needs or rights, or to foster the common good. We can identify as a structure of grace any cultural or social institution that enables people to express their love effectively, that fosters the common good, that counteracts selfishness, consumerism, individualism, or any other characteristic of society that works against the common good.

That institutions can also have negative characteristics is only too clear. As grace can and does inhere in institutions, so does its opposite; besides structures of grace there are structures of sin. Again, Richard McCormick:

> There has been a sea-change of moral consciousness during the past fifty years. During that period we gradually began to speak of sin not simply as the isolated act of an individual, but as having societal structural dimensions. We begin to see that the sins and selfishness of one generation became the inhibiting conditions of the next. The structures and institutions that oppress people, deprive them of rights and alienate them are embodiments of our sinful condition. The notion of systemic violence and social sin entered our vocabulary and is so much a part of it now that John Paul II uses it freely.[9]

An historical example of a sinful social structure in the history of the United States, one abolished more than a century ago but whose consequences are still felt in our society, is chattel slavery. It was based on atrocious beliefs, upheld by law, and embedded in economic structures. Even today those living in the United States must deal with a particular form of racism that is different from racism in other places because of our unique history.

Other sinful structures include promotion of smoking in poor countries as a way of compensating for profit loss due to declining smoking in other places, exploitative labor practices, and unjust tax laws. Just as it is possible to identify general characteristics of structures of grace, so we can name general characteristics and many other examples of structures of sin. Any social structure that encourages and rewards greed or selfishness is to that extent a structure of sin, as is any social structure that demeans human dignity or denies human rights, or promotes apathy about social responsibilities. Social structures are ordinarily not completely graced or completely sinful; still, there are many cases where either grace or sin is so predominant that one or the other label fits. In his encyclical letter *On Social Concern* (1987), Pope John Paul II wrote:

> The sum total of the negative factors working against a true awareness of the universal *common good*, and the need

to further it, gives the impression of creating, in persons and institutions, an obstacle difficult to overcome.

If the present situation can be attributed to difficulties of various kinds, it is not out of place to speak of "structures of sin," which, as I stated in my apostolic exhortation, *Reconciliatio et Paenitentia,* are rooted in personal sin, and thus always linked to the *concrete acts* of individuals who introduce these structures, consolidate them and make them difficult to remove. And thus they grow stronger, spread, and become the source of other sins, and so influence people's behavior. "Sin" and "structures of sin" are categories which are seldom applied to the situation of the contemporary world. However, one cannot easily gain a profound understanding of the reality that confronts us unless we give a name to the root of the evils which afflict us.[10]

What is the relationship of guilt to social structures of sin? Experience tells us that we are beneficiaries if not direct participants in many structures of sin. Most people in the United States eat food that is produced under unjust working conditions by migrant workers. Many of us wear clothing that is produced by foreign labor, including child labor, under conditions that violate basic justice. Many of us pay taxes, a huge proportion of which goes to maintain a military-industrial complex that includes kinds of weaponry and some practices that are clearly contrary to moral principles. The list of examples could be extended. We cannot act directly against all structures of sin all the time, but we are called to act responsibly on behalf of justice and peace within our capabilities. In the next two chapters we turn our attention to ways and means; first, however, we consider the matter of time.

Time and Social Change

"What time is it?" That simple question may be one of the most important questions we can ask. In some affairs, a sense of timing may be the critical factor that determines success or failure. In many human relationships—a marriage, a friendship, or a diplomatic negotiation, for example—there are decisive moments. In the preceding sections of this chapter we have explored dimensions of our lives mainly in spatial categories in order to get a sense of the structures within the societal sphere of our lives. Now we turn to a consideration of time in order to reach a deeper understanding and firmer commitment in the promotion of justice and peace.

Musing over the question of time in the context of U.S. foreign policy three months after the terrorist attacks on September 11, 2001, I asked myself, "What time is it?" and came up with the following list, certainly not complete and in no particular logical order:

What time is it? A time for endurance...a time for being attentive...a time for compassionate listening...a time for patience...a time for dialogue...a time for mourning...a time for awe...a time for courage...a time for mercy...a time for justice...a time for a fundamental option for poor people...a time for quiet, rest, silence...a time for generosity...a time to speak out...a time for trust.... a time for commitment...a time for gentleness...a time for self-control...a time for love...a time for wisdom...a time for peace...a time for knowledge...a time for compassion...a time for good judgment.

Our common sense experience of time is based on observation of the relationship of our Earth to the sun, moon, and stars and consistent measurement. Events begin at a certain time and have a middle and end according to calendar and clock. Some see in the introduction of the mechanical clock into Europe in the fourteenth century one of the most significant changes in Western civilization, which changed from being governed by planetary and biological rhythms to rhythms and measurements of time that seem to be under human control. This control pervades many dimensions of life. For example, in the lower echelons of an industrial economy workers are paid by the hour (a practice that raises the question why this is not true of the upper echelons).

Today we can recognize worldviews that are based on the way time is perceived or experienced. One view, expressed in such sayings as "That's the way things are," "History repeats itself," or "We've seen this before," sees time as relatively insignificant and regards much of reality as more or less stable and predictable. Another view is more keenly aware of the developmental and sometimes regressive quality of life experienced in time. Darwin's theory of evolution has had a profound effect on our sense of time as moving in a direction. Time as the ancient Greeks saw it was cyclical, endlessly repeating itself, while the Judeo-Christian view of time, in contrast, is linear, perceiving time as going somewhere, moving in a direction to a fullness we call the *parousia. Parousia* refers to the consummation of history in God, "the completeness on a cosmic scale of the process begun in the incarnation, death and resurrection of Christ."[11] In this view there is a notion of time, *kairos,* that is not chronological. *Kairos* introduces the notion of divine involvement and also of freedom in time. From the human perspective, *kairos* is time that calls for discernment and critical decision.

The Gospel of John portrays Jesus as acutely sensitive to *kairos.* In the episode of the wedding feast at Cana, where Mary approaches him about the shortage of wine, Jesus says to her, "Woman, what concern is that to you and to me? My hour has not yet come" (John 2:4). Later in the Gospel, as Jesus enters Jerusalem on the eve of his passion, he says, "The hour has come for the Son of Man to be glorified. Very truly, I tell you, unless a grain of wheat falls into the earth and dies, it remains just a single grain; but if it dies, it bears much fruit. Those who love their life lose it, and those who hate their life in this world will keep it for eternal life" (John 12:23–25).

As members of the church, which is the extension of Jesus Christ in historical time, our own time is meant to share in the quality of Jesus' own life in time. This means that we are called to participate in his work of redeeming the world from its slavery to all that hinders the freedom of the children of God. We share in the communion of saints. Cultivating relationships with members of the communion of saints is a source of energy for one's own life and work. I once asked Barbara Ward, the brilliant English econ-omist who played a significant role in the early days of the Pontifical Commission for Justice and Peace, how she was so able to grasp the meaning of wide sweeps of history and its import for the future. She told me that she thought about events in three time lines, or within three time frames: a year, ten years, and a hundred years. This can be a key to effective approaches to issues that are addressed by Catholic social teaching and by any move-ment or effort for justice and peace. Situating a problem within this threefold framework can help one come to an understanding of the different kinds of action called for and the qualities needed for these actions.

Finally, a Christian lives with an eye on a future beyond calculation. Karl Rahner, in an essay about Advent, wrote:

> If we do not look toward the future, we basically do not know at all what the meaning and purpose of the present task is. Advent summons us to look to the future and to plan something for the day after tomorrow, trusting in the conviction that if our plan for the near future should collapse, we have still survived the near future with courage against shortsighted resignation and we have demonstrated that we have faith in the eternal future of God....We should really ask ourselves in complete intimacy and concreteness if the spirit and heart in us still have a little room for novelty and future beyond the present.[12]

A wise friend once told me that the question "What time is it?" appeared to him more and more as perhaps the most important question to be asked in making a decision. This presumes sensitivity to the signs of the times, to the deep involvement of God in time, and to the mystery and wonder that we live in the fullness of time. Again, Karl Rahner: "As Christians see and experience it, the present already bears the future within itself. And the eternal future of God is already the force and the power in the midst of the present."[13]

Paying Attention to Issues of Justice and Peace

When faced with issues of economic and political injustice, or simply with issues of economic, social, and political complexity, many people feel overwhelmed and tempted simply to ignore them on the grounds that there is nothing we can do about them, or to blame the system. In the United States, several cultural factors play into the temptation to excuse ourselves from involvement. We are a highly individualistic people with myths and traditions about the self-made individual who can do anything he or she sets out to do. If we are not on our guard, we tend to blame the victim when we hear about the plight of people who are poor. Blaming the victim is easier than carefully analyzing the situation.

The particular problem—loss of a job, for example—is frequently related to large issues beyond the control of the individual worker or employer. While this seems obvious, it is more easily said than accepted by a person who is out of work. So strongly is a sense of self-worth and identity linked to material well-being in our society that the unemployed person easily feels a failure even where there is no personal failure. Coupled with anxiety, this is a recipe for all kinds of personal and social ills.

Treating symptoms is not enough. While collections for the needy give comfort and alleviate pain by responding to symptoms and providing short-term help, they do not get directly at the causes of problems. This fact should not be used as a rationale for ignoring the immediate needs of those suffering. Service given with love is absolutely necessary. This is particularly true of love that costs, as in the case of those who give their lives lovingly to the care of the most abandoned day after day. Besides directly helping those in need, this kind of loving service keeps society in touch with the deepest dimension and value of life. It is unwarranted to criticize those who are meeting immediate needs because they are not at the same time working directly to change structures. When those who meet immediate needs do this well, they are bringing the truths of the gospel to bear on culture. They are evangelizing the culture, and in this way contributing to a change of structures, although this may not be immediately evident.

What practical conclusions are to be drawn from this linkage between the personal and systemic? Those not immediately facing problems of basic human need, like finding remunerative work to pay the necessary bills, are called to work for just economic policies that determine the scope of individual action. Economic policies do not happen; they are human constructions and need to be continually scrutinized from the perspective of justice. Apathy on the part of many is a recipe for a lopsided economy where too few control most of the wealth and the political power that goes with it. No society can be a just one unless a critical mass of its members commit themselves to the common good, know what kinds of policies are needed, and translate their commitment to action.

Today the local economy, wherever we live, is inextricably linked to a global economy. The food we eat, the clothes we wear, almost everything else in our daily lives has some connection to workers in other parts of the world. The division of labor today is in many respects international. When questions about the conditions and consequences of trade, debt, employment practices, and conditions are not faced, the poor and weak are thereby abandoned to those who view them as no more than tools of production to be used, used up, and discarded. In *Economic Justice for All*, the bishops of the United States gave us clear normative questions for assessing an economic system in which specific issues are contained. They wrote:

> Does our economic system place more emphasis on maximizing profits than on meeting human needs and fostering human dignity? Does our economy distribute its benefits equitably or does it concentrate power and resources in the hands of a few? Does it promote excessive materialism and individualism? Does it adequately protect the environment and the nation's natural resources? Does it direct too many scarce resources to military purposes? These and other basic questions about the economy need to be scrutinized in light of the ethical norms we have outlined. We urge continuing exploration of these systemic questions in a more comprehensive way than this document permits.[14]

In the next two chapters we carry these questions with us as we examine several tested methods of working for social change.

QUESTIONS FOR STUDY, REFLECTION, AND CONVERSATION

1. Do you agree that "today there is a growing sense that we belong to the Earth before we belong to any other group or community" (p. 101)?
2. Give examples of the cultural shift described by Sandra Schneiders on page 102.
3. Discuss the relationship between terrorism and war. Is terrorism a particular kind of war? Is war a particular kind of terrorism?

4. "War on terrorism" is generally accepted in the United States as necessary. Do you agree that it is time for a war on terrorism? Can you think of alternative policies and strategies?

5. *Solidarity* is proposed as a word for the love that unites personal and social action. How is solidarity related to active nonviolence?

6. Give examples of structures of grace and structures of sin in which you are personally involved. How do you understand your responsibilities? Be specific.

7. Review the U.S. bishops' set of questions for assessing an economic system from a moral perspective (p. 113). Would you add, change, or delete any of the questions? Why?

NOTES

1. David Toolan, *At Home in the Cosmos* (Maryknoll, NY: Orbis, 2001), 188.

2. Brian Swimme and Thomas Berry, *The Universe Story: From the Primordial Flaring Forth to the Ecozoic Era–A Celebration of the Unfolding of the Cosmos* (New York: HarperCollins, 1992), 243.

3. Ibid.

4. Sandra M. Schneiders, *With Oil in their Lamps: Faith, Feminism, and the Future* (New York/Mahwah, NJ: Paulist Press, 2000), 50–51.

5. Martin Luther King Jr., in *Peacemaking: Day by Day* (Erie, PA: Pax Christi USA, 1985), 126.

6. *Sollicitudo Rei Socialis,* arts. 38–39, pp. 421–22, in David J. O'Brien and Thomas A. Shannon, eds., *Catholic Social Thought: The Documentary Heritage* (Maryknoll, NY: Orbis, 1992).

7. Pope John Paul II, World Day of Peace Message 2001, "Dialogue between Cultures for a Civilization of Love and Peace," art. 18, *Origins* 30 (29), January 4, 2001: 462–63.

8. Richard A. McCormick, SJ, *Corrective Vision: Explorations in Moral Theology* (Kansas City, MO: Sheed and Ward, 1994), 63–64.

9. Ibid., 18.

10. *Sollicitudo Rei Socialis,* art. 36, pp. 419–20.

11. Zachary Hayes, OFM, "Parousia," in Joseph A. Komonchak, Mary Collins, and Dermot A. Lane, eds., *A New Dictionary of Theology* (Collegeville, MN: Liturgical Press, 1991), 743.

12. Karl Rahner, *The Great Church Year: The Best of Karl Rahner's Homilies, Sermons, and Meditations,* ed. Albert Raffelt, trans. ed. Harvey D. Egan, SJ (New York: Crossroad, 1993), 9.

13. Ibid., 10.

14. *Economic Justice for All,* art. 132, p. 610, in O'Brien and Shannon, *Catholic Social Thought.*

CHAPTER NINE

Methods of Social Change

Imagination is more important than knowledge.
—Albert Einstein

CHAPTER FOCUS

Work for social change requires some understanding of the complexities of social institutions and systems, and also some coherent methods for influencing institutions. Social analysis is a problem-solving method that follows a recurring pattern, including description and analysis of a problem, reflection, planning, carrying out the planned action, and evaluation. A second method, imaging a preferred future, begins by imagining in detail a desired outcome and then incorporating analysis in describing how the preferred outcome might be accomplished. Both methods are ideally group processes, though individuals can benefit from practicing them in a modified way.

Introduction

The following passage from the landmark document *Justice in the World* succinctly expresses the dynamics of a social spirituality:

> According to St. Paul, the whole of the Christian life is summed up in faith effecting that love and service of neighbor which involve the fulfillment of the demands of justice. The Christian lives under the interior law of liberty, which is a permanent call to man [each person] to turn away from self-sufficiency to confidence in God and from concern for self to a sincere love of neighbor. Thus

takes place his [our] genuine liberation and the gift of himself [ourselves] for the freedom of others.[1]

This chapter describes two ways of living this spirituality in work for institutional change. These two ways can equip us to deal realistically with the enormity and complexity of institutions and systems that affect our lives. Working with others we can help to bring about constructive change in such institutions as the health care system, the government, or the intricacies of economic and financial institutions, among others.

Organizing for Justice and Peace

Institutions depend on role relationships. If the police are doing their work properly, we do not care whether we know them on a first-name basis. If things are going well in our town, we are quite content if we are not the mayor's friend. Role relationships are governed by unwritten rules of civility and by moral laws of truthfulness, respect, and justice. Justice as a fundamental virtue in the societal dimension is expressed in relationships in which all members of a society have their needs met as a matter of right, and not at the pleasure of individuals or groups who have arbitrary power over others. At the heart of social justice is a fundamental undertow of love, that is, basic good will toward the other and desire to make that good will effective.

A major problem of our time is the growth of international institutions, corporations, and conglomerates that have far more material resources than many states. This is especially problematic for poor countries, many of them former colonial powers with little political power in international negotiations. Today, many of the most powerful institutions in the world are commercial corporations that wield enormous power internationally. No international government can hold these corporations accountable. The driving force of commercial corporations is the increase of profits in competition with other corporations. It is extremely difficult to contain this drive within the boundaries of the common good, and consequently the gap between the rich and poor continues to grow.

Dorothy Day liked to repeat that we are called to build the new in the shell of the old. The place to begin to do this is in those local social structures in which we spend our lives, particularly in the family, the local parish community, neighborhood organizations of civil society, and educational institutions at all levels. These are intermediate structures between the individual and the larger institutions, where we can shape and maintain those values that are the deep foundation of society. In this way we help form and maintain the culture of justice and peace.

Justice and peace organizations are found on the local, national, and international levels.[2] They enable the individual to join forces with like-minded people who support each other in effective action that no individual could accomplish alone. In this way they provide constructive alternatives to injustice and violence. By supporting, and in some cases by becoming members of justice and peace organizations, we can find resources for the methods of social change described in this chapter. The next chapter briefly describes a few of these organizations.

Two Methods of Working Together for Social Change

We now look at two ways of working to change institutions. One of these is primarily a "left-brain" method that highlights analytic processes. The other method is primarily a "right-brain" way that accents functions of imagination and intuition, although it incorporates much analytic work as well. Ideally, methods of social change employ all these functions; however, in practice not everything can be done at once, nor all things equally well by every individual.

Both methods presuppose a motivated group committed to a sustained process. In the absence of a group, either of these methods can be used in some form by a single individual, but it will probably not be possible for a person to take all the action steps seen as necessary. In order to translate plans into actions, ordinarily there must be a gathering of persons around an idea or an issue or deeply held values.

In explaining the structure of social institutions in chapter 7, I used the analogy of physical anatomy and identified eight constitutive parts of a social institution. Continuing the analogy, we recognize that just as a doctor must also know how the body functions—that is, understand physiology—we need to know how social institutions function in their particular environment. This is more challenging than simply identifying an institution's eight constitutive parts. Institutions are as unique as persons. Like persons, they have a history that affects their laws and customs as well as their beliefs and values. Further, it is hardly possible to touch one part of an institution without affecting every other part, because the parts are functionally interdependent. For example, if communication in a society falls victim to a pattern of lies from the government, communication among the populace will be colored by cynicism. Eventually people will lose their basic respect for the government, thus changing some of their fundamental political attitudes and beliefs. Some individuals play stellar roles in institutional change; however, other people who do not make the headlines may play more important roles that go unnoticed. We often know so much about those who have the leading roles that we can all too easily underestimate the supporting cast. This is not to downplay the importance of leaders, but to remind us of their dependence on many others who do not win the attention of journalists or historians.

Far-reaching change for the better, change that is sustained and developmental, is frequently brought about by movements that begin as small groups in which the members know one another personally. They begin to forge bonds that depend less on roles than on shared values and a shared goal. If their shared goal is compelling, and if what needs to be done is sufficiently demanding, these relationships may develop into a social movement, and eventually into an organization, that is, into an institution. There is an old French saying that institutions destined to have long lives have ancestors but no birthdays. History may later assign a starting date for the sake of celebrating anniversaries, but the real story as known by those who were a part of an institution from the start usually includes not one event but a number of signal events at the beginning of the institution.

An understanding of the broader history and culture of the society in which the institution is located is essential for effective institutional development. Without this broader knowledge, dialogue at sufficient depth is impeded. Dialogue may well be the single most important tool for social development. It depends on the capacity to listen and to be sensitive to others' feelings and understanding of their values and beliefs, as well as on the capacity to communicate about values even more than about particular issues. Institutions flourish when those who make up the institution nurture their most important values and beliefs; institutions languish, decline, and decay when their members neglect to do this. A social institution that forgets its original reason for existence may end up spending its energies primarily on its own survival. If this happens, the institution is moving toward collapse.

Social Analysis

Social analysis,[3] as described below, is a six-step method; only one of which is analysis proper. The first step is to *describe the problem or issue* to be analyzed. The members of the group recount their experiences of the problem under consideration, describing as fully as they can all they know about the institutional aspects of the problem. The problem may be a local issue—for example, neighborhood violence, the closing of a major business or industry in the area, poor schools, or dumping toxic waste; or the group may focus on a broader issue, such as military spending, access to affordable health care, or immigration policy. In either case, the history of the problem is researched, preferably by several members of the group. Group discussion helps distinguish verifiable facts from opinions or impressions unsupported by evidence. Vague statements or broad generalizations are also questioned, sometimes noted for further investigation. This first step, description of the issue and its history, may take several meetings of the group. More is going on than learning about the issue; the members are also coming to know each other better and are improving their communication skills.

In the second step, analysis proper, the group *identifies both those who have principal roles in the institution as well as those who work behind the scenes.* For example, a school principal may be blamed for something decided at a higher level by a school superintendent whose name and precise function are not known to the group at the beginning of the process of social analysis. The analysis aims for the identification of cause and effect relationships in the data gathered in the first step of the process. At this stage it can be helpful to consider the eight constitutive parts of an institution described in chapter 7 and to examine each in turn. For example, what are the expressed beliefs and values of the institution? Are they consistent with the behavior of the institution? What about the laws and regulations? Are they clear? Out of date? Are there some practices for which there are no norms or clear guidelines? Are the laws or regulations discriminatory? In favor of whom? Against whom? Each of the constitutive parts of the institution can be similarly examined. At all times the group tries to keep clearly in mind the purpose of the social analysis and to avoid personal attacks or any other behavior that could easily damage the process. This is not easy when those involved may have suffered injustice and have very strong feelings and a personal stake in the outcome of the process.

The third step is to *reflect, judge, and decide to act.* This is not done in a vacuum. For some it will entail theological reflection; for others, philosophical. In either case, the effort is to look at the situation in light of the group's deepest values and beliefs. For example, the economic data and analysis can be measured by the criteria of love and justice, with attention to the impact of economic decisions on poor people. We ask whether poor people have access not only to goods but also to decision making in matters that affect them.

Theological reflection grounded in Christian faith and prayer helps us to be mindful of our relationship with Jesus Christ and the communion of saints, prophets, and witnesses to which we belong. Such reflection engenders hope and encourages us to take risks when we are working for and with persons whose well-being is entrusted to us. In reflection and prayer we come to know, over and over again, that we can leave the matter of visible success or failure in God's hands. In some cases we can realistically expect our efforts for social justice to effect major changes within our lifetime, while in others we may not live to see the completion of our efforts. We know that our vocation is to be faithful. "Plant a vineyard for your children, and an olive grove for your grandchildren." This ancient Greek proverb is relevant to social change efforts in our own day, as is another wise observation, that when people plant trees under which they know they themselves will never sit, civilization has come to that land.

The fourth step is to *make a plan for action* with objectives, strategies, and procedures, and clear delineation of responsibilities and accountability. If the first three steps have been done well, we can expect strong motivation when it comes to formulating the plan of action and a high level of ownership of the undertaking. For this step the group can use an outline such as the following:

Goals: What are the desired outcomes of this effort?

Objectives: What are the measurable accomplishments we will attempt? Within what time frame?

Strategies: How will we achieve the objectives? What specific steps or actions will the group undertake?

Procedures: What are the specific assignments for individuals in the group? What are the lines of accountability? What is the plan for communication during the project? What is the plan for evaluation?

The fifth step is to *take the action that has been planned,* and the sixth is to *review and evaluate the action.* Depending on the nature and scope of the activity, the group may want outside help for this last step. Evaluation can help the group appreciate lessons learned and can show possible next steps.

This method of social analysis is illustrated by Figure 6. Social analysis is meant to be an ascending spiral. The situation in which the process began will have changed, partly because of the group's actions, and also because of other factors outside the group. Society is dynamic and can always be improved.

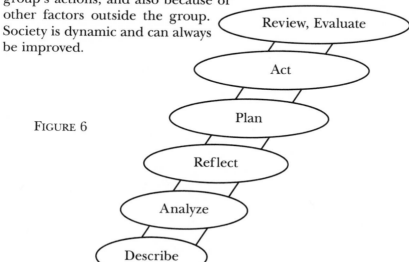

FIGURE 6

Imaging a Preferred Future

Work for peace and justice is often done in a situation of conflict or hostility. The situation may be a very personal matter—for example, the attempt to heal a wounded friendship—or it may be an international affair, for example, an effort to forestall a war looming on the horizon. Whatever the issue, we will be trying to create an alternative future. In the method of social analysis described, experience confirms that a restored or healed friendship may be stronger than the original relationship because the friends will be wiser, more humble, more grateful and appreciative of the gift of friendship that they may previously have taken for granted. In the second example, a war prevented provides social and political space for developing nonviolent ways of dealing with other conflicts that were at the root of the threatened war.

Creative imagination can play a large role in effective work for justice and peace, putting us in touch with the past as memory and the future as possibility and hope. When imagination is centered on the future, it is not reproducing images of the past but creating something new. Human development, both personal and social, depends on imagination. Scientists and artists spend days, even years imagining possibilities and then testing their hypotheses and images with experiments.[4]

History is a succession of imagined events. If we agree with Einstein that imagination is more important than knowledge, we want to know the difference between creative imagination and mere fantasy, and how to cultivate imagination. Imagination is about making things real, about embodying the abstract in images. Such images have strong power to move us, a power stronger than abstract concepts, important as concepts are. Victor Hugo stated an important truth when he said that nothing is so powerful as an idea whose time has come. This kind of idea is generated from images and expressed in new images as well as in concepts.

Fred Polak, a Dutch sociologist who did important work on the place of imagination in social reconstruction after World War II, taught that positive images that propel constructive change do not just happen. Rather, they flourish in an atmosphere that places a high value on creative imagination together with philosophical questioning, a rich emotional life, and freedom of speech and fantasy. Further, he held, the potential strength of a culture could actually be measured by the intensity, energy, and belief in its images of the future. The force that generates images is only partly a matter of reason; emotion plays a crucial role.[5]

Positive, constructive images have been described as prophetic and poetic, showing possibilities or alternatives of what might be. Scientists who make breakthroughs often work with this kind of image. Such images are intuitive insights by which a person grasps the big picture of a possibility. Motivated by this intuitive, imaginative grasp, the scientist can then endure the long labor of working out details. Something similar works for the artist who holds in the mind's eye or ear a scene or theme that propels the next steps.

Prophetic images rouse emotion and have power to move others. They give us the expectancies and beliefs that motivate action. Leaders who can create and sustain social movements are gifted with this kind of imagination. Martin Luther King Jr. is a good example. The images and emotions evoked in his "I Have a Dream" speech continue to exercise a strong power in the United States and beyond. Another example is the Statue of Liberty in New York harbor. This sculptured image acts not only as inspiration but also as a critique when policies and practices violate the values embodied in the image. A cluster of images that are consistent with each other tends to be self-fulfilling. A group of people who construct such images over a period of time through formal and/or informal processes will want to make their images real in society.

Hand in hand with creative imagination is the capacity to appreciate, to admire, to be grateful for goodness already present. Appreciation and gratitude evoke a feeling for the goodness and desirability of an imaged future. The appreciative person sees the hidden reality deep below the surface and evokes possibilities. Appreciation is at the heart of artistic production, whether the artist is working in stone, at a word processor, or as an artist teacher working with the potential of the developing person at any age. Appreciation involves seeing through a loving, caring lens; it is love responding to potential as well as to immediate need.

Exercises in Imaging a Preferred Future

The following set of exercises[6] has been adapted from workshops organized for those involved in peace work, but they can also be used for community organizers, urban planners, and many others. Some of the exercises can be used in modified form by individuals, but the entire set of exercises is designed for groups of between twelve and twenty-five members. The exercises include a mix of individual and group work. Each step is an integral part of the process and builds on the steps preceding it.

This set of exercises can be done by a group with very mixed backgrounds, though it presupposes in the context of this book some general desire to know more about the possibilities of promoting justice and peace in some way. If the group shares a common faith, it will be able to draw on rich religious experience and symbols. In this case time is provided for both personal and common prayer and theological reflection. If the exercises are done in a secular context, the facilitator sets a reflective tone supportive of profound experience that is almost invariably part of the process.

It is a serious process, not to be entered into as light recreation. At the same time, as the process develops there is typically an experience of high energy, humor, and joy. The process requires sufficient time in order to work well. Ordinarily an imaging workshop is conducted during three or more consecutive days. The sessions may be spread over a longer period, for example, an evening each week for several months. The process requires a facilitator who gives the group the following directions for each exercise and keeps the group on track. (Note that the facilitator's directions are given in direct address. Nothing should be omitted, though the wording may be adapted to a particular group.)

1. *Goal setting.* In preparation for the first group session, each of you is to write a goal or goals for a year thirty years from the present. Make this a social goal, that is, some cultural or institutional achievement you would like to see thirty years from now. Be concrete and specific. For example, "world peace" is not an appropriate goal for this process because it is too general; "international agreement to destroy nuclear arsenals" is an appropriate goal. "Elimination of global poverty" is not a realistic goal; " international agreements to eliminate exploitative child labor" is a realistic goal.

Be as hopeful as you can in this goal statement, and do not be concerned about the ways and means or the obstacles on the way to the goal. That will come later in the process. Throughout the imaging workshop you may modify your goal as you interact with others. It is important to keep a goal in sight throughout the entire process as a way of keeping a clear focus and as a reality check. Share your goal with two or three others. This will be done during the workshop, but it can also be done informally between workshop sessions. (The facilitator schedules time for writing personal goals and for sharing with others.)

2. *Memory exercise.* The next exercise also has two parts, individual work followed by sharing, this time with one other person. Recall in as much detail as you can some experience of your early life that you genuinely appreciated. It need not be an experience of long duration. Perhaps it was a particular hug that put the world together at a time it seemed to be collapsing when you were only four or five years old. Whatever it was, it is important to take time to relive this experience in your memory, particularly to bring back the good emotions connected with the experience. Notice if details begin to present themselves, whether of sights or sounds or even smells associated with the experience. Next, share your memory with a partner and listen to your partner's memory. (Note: The facilitator may notice that when this sharing is done by all participants in a large room, with everyone speaking softly, ordinarily an unmistakable atmosphere of joy and deep feeling permeates the atmosphere. At the end of the exercise the facilitator may call to the attention of the group that the participants have been using imagination. This may help overcome resistance of any participants who may think they have no imagination or are resistant to using it.)

3. *Visiting the future.* This exercise is done alone and will take some time. Move imaginatively into a place thirty years from now that corresponds to your goal. Walk around, look and see, listen and hear, touch and feel. Imaginatively converse with people you meet on your walk. Travel as far as you want or need to travel, or stay close to home. Go where your imagination takes you, corresponding to your goal. Imagine first, then record what you imagine. Use present tense. You are in the year 20—. Do not ask how your imaginative future came about. That will come later.

Now you are simply to be part of the scene. Be there, be specific. Record images, pictures, symbols, unconnected words, diagrams. There are many areas to investigate for your 20— scenario. Ask questions of the imagined people you see in order to understand more clearly. Let the movie unreel in your imagination. Unlike a movie, you can question the characters. Always use the present tense. You are there, in a future that is now. From time to time look at your goal and hopes. Be sure that your imagined scenario incorporates the goal that you wrote back in 20—. Keep asking questions of the characters in the scenario under discussion. Look for relationships, significant persons, and so on. What are children, women, men doing? Describe household groupings, buildings, workplaces, and such. Begin with those aspects that interest you most. How are conflicts handled? How are goods produced and distributed? What is the government like on various levels? What is your parish like?

4. *Sharing scenarios.* Now in groups of three persons share your scenarios, each person in turn without interruption. After each sharing, the two listeners are to ask questions for clarification. In answering, the person who shared the scenario may well find that more details will develop. Be sure to use the present tense when describing your scenario. (The facilitator moves among the groups and reminds those who slip into the past or future to use the present tense. This is very important.)

After the sharing, go back to the drawing board. Make a simple sketch of your scenario, including new ideas that developed during the sharing process. (The facilitator provides large pieces of paper and markers in a variety of colors.) You don't need to be an artist. Use simple stick figures, or if necessary, key words, but don't write out a story. Next hang up your poster and walk around and study the other posters. Put your name on those that show scenarios to which you feel attracted. (On the basis of this signing, the facilitator forms groups of four or five persons who will then develop group scenarios that incorporate some of the ideas from each person in the group.)

5. *Developing group scenarios.* Your group of four or five persons is now to develop one scenario for 20— that can be owned by the group. This will require a good bit of explaining to each other, and also compromise. It is well worth the effort. The scenario will reflect the richness that comes from the creativity and effort of all the members. Make a list of the elements that you want in your common scenario. This list will be used as a reference as you

develop your poster. As far as possible use images and symbols; use words only when necessary for the group poster. You will use words later, when your group presents the scenario to all the other groups. Do not try to solve all the problems and answer all the ways and means questions in this exercise. That will come later. Typically, groups devise interesting ways to present their scenario to the group. Be creative in preparing your presentation, possibly as a one-act play, an interview, a presentation to a congressional committee, and so on.

6. *Group presentation of scenarios.* Each small working group presents its scenario and answers questions about it. Again, details will develop in this process as the creativity of the group increases.

7. *Writing a history of the future.* All the time you have been working, you have been reminded to speak in the present tense. By this time you probably feel some genuine belief in the scenario, the imagined reality that your small group has created. Now you are about to write the history of the scenario you have developed. First, each member of the small working group writes a brief account of how the scenario came to be. To do this, move back from the scenario about five years at a time and tell what had happened by that date to make the end result a reality. You need not be strict about the five-year segments. What is important is to describe in some detail elements of the development process that led to the scenario. What were the political developments in the thirty-year period? Economic changes? Changes in education? Scientific breakthroughs? Cultural achievements? When did they occur? Were there any crises during the thirty-year period? What were they? Next, the members of the working group come together to construct one history of their future scenario, using elements from the histories they constructed individually.

8. *Group presentation of history.* Each small group explains its history of the future to the entire group and answers questions. You will notice that as the history moves back closer to the present, it reveals actions that need to be taken now and in the very near future. The history is to be recounted from the goal, thirty years hence, back to the present, not from the present to the goal.

9. *Develop a plan of action.* Each participant now works privately with questions about immediate action steps that seem important for realization of the imagined future. Think about such questions as these:

> In light of my intended future,
> What are my short-term objectives? Which are most
>   important?
> What are my long-term objectives?
> How are short- and long-term objectives linked?
> Who will be allies and supporters?
> What are some obstacles?
> How will I deal with these?
> How will I hold myself accountable?
> What resources do I have? What resources do I need
>   to develop?

Decide what part of your action plan you want to share with the group. Finally, write your action plan, and keep it with your goal.

QUESTIONS FOR STUDY, REFLECTION, AND CONVERSATION

1. How do you understand Dorothy Day's idea of building the new in the shell of the old?
2. Why is social analysis ideally done by a group?
3. Why is it important to know the history of an organization we want to influence?
4. Describe action planning, the fourth step in social analysis, as it might be applied to one of your personal goals.
5. Do you think that imagination gets enough attention in working for justice and peace?
6. Discuss the possibility of forming a group to practice either or both of the methods for promoting social change described in this chapter.

NOTES

1. *Justice in the World,* 293, in David J. O'Brien and Thomas A. Shannon, eds., *Catholic Social Thought: The Documentary Heritage* (Maryknoll, NY: Orbis, 1992).

2. Jackie Smith, Charles Chatfield, and Ron Pagnucco, eds., *Transnational Social Movements and Global Politics: Solidarity beyond the State* (Syracuse, NY: Syracuse University Press, 1997), chapters 1–4.

3. Joe Holland and Peter Henriot, SJ, *Social Analysis: Linking Faith and Justice,* rev. and enl. ed. (Maryknoll, NY: Orbis, 1983). This remains a useful guide. See pp. 95–106, "Social Analysis: A Practical Methodology."

4. Elise Boulding, *Building a Global Civic Culture: Education for an Interdependent World* (Syracuse, NY: Syracuse University Press, 1988), chapter 6, "Uses of the Imagination."

5. Ibid., 110.

6. The exercises in imaging a preferred future are based on Boulding, *Building a Global Culture,* 172–76.

CHAPTER TEN

— ✤ —

Service in Justice and Peace

It is not enough to recall principles,
state intentions, point to crying injustices,
and utter prophetic denunciations;
these words will lack real weight unless
they are accompanied for each individual by a livelier
awareness of personal responsibility and by effective action.
—Pope Paul VI, *A Call to Action*

CHAPTER FOCUS

Seven ways of acting for social change discussed in this chapter correspond to various personality types and preferred ways of working. Understanding these different ways can help an individual find a preferred way or ways. This understanding can also contribute to mutual appreciation and support of others in efforts for justice and peace. Today, ecumenical and interfaith dialogue and cooperation in social action is increasingly important. Many organized peace and justice movements, some of which are briefly described in this chapter, enable individuals to collaborate and to multiply their effectiveness. An understanding of the creative tension between movements and organizations is a help in understanding one important dynamic of social change.

Seven Ways to Work for Justice and Peace

Our actions do make a difference. Society is not static, a fixed product of remote social forces, but at any given moment is a product of the behavior of those who enjoy its benefits, suffer from its inadequacies, and contribute to its flourishing or to its

decline. The question is not whether our actions make a difference, but what kind of actions we should undertake. We consider
seven ways of social action viewed from the perspective of the *person,* rather than from the perspective of particular issues. This may
help us come to an understanding of how we can best use our particular gifts and talents. Each of these ways is effective. Our task is
to choose the way or ways in which we can work well. That will
depend on a number of factors, including age and strength,
knowledge and skill, and time.

The following seven ways of working for peace and justice are
not meant to be an exhaustive list. They correspond to various talents and capacities and all of them are probably present in groups
of any size. By recognizing them in others we can learn to affirm
their strengths and discover our own and not expect the same
kinds of action from everyone.

1. *Reminding.* First, there is the way of reminding. It is difficult to focus on issues of poverty and injustice. In the media, it is
sometimes hard to distinguish among news, analysis, opinion,
entertainment, and advertising. The popular media has a strong
tendency to keep at a distance or treat superficially poor people
and those who suffer. A story about a famine or a bombing raid
may be followed immediately by a commercial about a vacation
cruise. It is reasonable to suspect that this pattern viewed over and
over again has a negative effect on human awareness and sensitivity to human suffering.

In the service of reminding, we can keep significant issues
before ourselves and others in many constructive ways. We can
bring issues up in conversation and contact our representatives in
government by letters, phone calls, and visits. Some people make
friends with the editor of their parish bulletin and supply short
pieces, including brief quotations from Catholic social teaching, to
help educate the parish community about the teaching of the
church on social issues. The service of reminding, of keeping the
poor on the agenda in constructive ways, is open to all of us. It is
a genuine way of telling the good news that God has not abandoned the poor but has entrusted them to us.

2. *Interpreting.* Second is the ministry of interpreting. Putting
issues on the agenda is indispensable, but this is only the begin-

ning. To work for social change requires understanding the background of an issue, as well as the various steps in social analysis. The ministry of interpreting is especially appropriate for those with talent in teaching or writing. Many people get their information about social issues from sketchy and often inaccurate accounts in the media. To provide more adequate information and analysis is a much needed service.

Think of issues affecting children, for example. The Children's Defense Fund has helped educate the public about the plight of poor children in the United States and the causes of their poverty. Less attention is given to poor children in poor countries, many of whom are victims of war, while others spend their school-age years working under deplorable conditions in factories. Children in such situations are voiceless and helpless in their oppression unless someone takes up their cause. There are effective organizational ways to help children by interpreting their situation for those who are unaware of the conditions in which many children live. Through organizational channels, people can bring information to the local level, disseminate it more widely, and shape it for particular audiences; in short, they can act as interpreters for the small and the voiceless.

Through practice, interpreters learn how to speak effectively to groups and how to write to be read. They follow an issue over a period of time, study the literature on it, and come to know resource persons and organizations that deal with the issue. People who do this are contributing to a community of concern and expertise, and in this way they help tilt the balance of society in the direction of goodness and justice and peace. Social change works from the grassroots up; movements that have brought about far-reaching change are often coalitions of poor and nonpoor people working together. There is deep satisfaction in this work, and much of it comes from the companions on the journey.

3. *Advocating.* A third way of service is advocating, which often flows directly from interpreting. Political strategies come immediately to mind. This was brought home to me in the early days of Bread for the World, the Christian citizens' movement that lobbies on behalf of close to a billion hungry people worldwide, more than half of them children. I was on Bread for the World's educational staff when the organization was just beginning. At the

seminars we held throughout the United States in order to help ordinary citizens become citizen lobbyists, participants did much role playing, some acting as advocates before other seminar participants who played the role of congressperson. They talked about such issues as food stamps, international food reserves as insurance against disasters, and other hunger-related issues. Participants in these seminars were often very diffident when they began. Some had never written a letter on a political issue and in many cases had never visited their congressional representatives when they were home in their districts. In the months following the series of seminars, some participants told us that their legislators thanked them for information about aspects of hunger issues that influenced the way they voted.

Peace and justice advocates who live in a democratic society have access to their elected representatives who are accountable to the people they represent. When legislators do not use their power to bring about constructive change, it is sometimes because they do not know enough about a particular issue. Given the range of issues that national or even state legislators must face, this is not surprising. Many citizen advocates learn that their representatives are genuinely grateful to learn from those who are either directly involved in an issue or have invested time in studying it. It is not always politicians' fault when they do not act wisely. We live in a complex world in which specialization is necessary. Competence has power to move others because the competent, well-informed person is credible in his or her area of specialization. By becoming competent in some social issues we can become effective, credible advocates. To help the individual citizen advocate, there are organizations such as Network and Center of Concern that do high-quality research and analysis and communicate it in ways that are understandable to the nonspecialist. These organizations have earned the respect of policymakers by their record of careful analysis.

Advocacy with local and state governments and with corporations on behalf of justice issues is important. For advocacy work related to corporations, individuals can work together through the Interfaith Center for Corporate Responsibility. This effective organization helps its members use their rights as shareholders to advocate on particular issues. Those who are not shareholders in a particular company can be effective consumer advocates when they act together in well-organized campaigns. For example, as the result of organized advocacy, two of the largest toy store chains, one of them international, announced that they were removing realistic-looking toy assault weapons from their shelves. Many people who had campaigned against war toys for years saw their efforts rewarded.

4. *Resisting.* A fourth way of working for peace and justice is resisting, which is the other side of advocating. Where advocacy is inspired by a good to be achieved, resistance is a direct response to evil. The first act of resistance is to name the evil. The case of slavery in U.S. history is a classic case. Abolitionists named and resisted slavery as evil for centuries while many who held positions of leadership in church and state were silent or made efforts to justify what we now recognize as a great moral evil. An important form of resistance is conscientious objection to military service based on religious or philosophical conviction. Nonviolent civil disobedience is still another important form of resistance when it is accompanied by clear expression of the reasons for refusing to obey. When judges forbid those charged with civil disobedience the opportunity to explain their actions, they witness to their own recognition of the potential of reasonable speech to expose an evil.

Resistance sometimes begins with a small minority, even a minority of one, and the resister may pay a very high price. A notable example is Saint Thomas More, who was the king's good servant but God's first. Saint Thomas More lost his life for his resistance to the king's claim to be the supreme head of the church of England. Examples of heroic resistance closer to our time include leaders of Christian base communities and labor organizers killed within recent memory in Central America. The service of resistance calls for careful discernment, self-knowledge, honesty, and courage. Resisters are wise when they seek a supportive community and blessed when they find or found one. At times they may find themselves alone.

5. *Caring.* A fifth mode of peace and justice service is caring. This is easier to recognize than to describe. To care is to love attentively with genuine practical concern for the other's needs. Imagine what would become of international affairs if armies all over the world taught their recruits that the first thing they must learn and practice is to care for all those they would meet in their

work at home and abroad. We have been born into a world with an adversarial view of human nature, a view fostered by history books that have glorified courage in battle against enemies much more than they have treated many other dimensions of history. Most human activity that has kept the human race here all these years has been caring activity, of parents for children, farmers for the land, craftspeople for their tools and the work of their hands, and many other kinds of caring activity. To contribute to a culture of caring, flowing from respect for our Creator and for all creation, is to be a peacemaker of a high order.[1]

6. *Fostering community.* Closely related to caring is fostering community, a sixth way of service for peace and justice. Peace and justice are qualities of good relationships. Community is different from a mere group. A community presupposes some shared experiences, shared ideas, and shared values, and ultimately genuine love, the desire for one another's true good. Those who are able to bring people together and to keep them together around an important issue or cause are essential to the work of justice and peacemaking. Because no one person will have all the needed skills or the time required for this work, it is important to be able to recognize our own and others' particular gifts and to contribute to the common task. At times this may be something as mundane as making phone calls or coffee, or taking the minutes at a meeting. It will also mean laboring to express an idea clearly so that it can be examined by the group, gathering data, or raising money. Some people spend a great deal of time and energy looking for a community that shares their values and concerns and fail to find one. In such a situation, a saying to remember is, "If you can't find it, found it." Many a long-lived peace and justice community as well as large movements and organizations began with a very small group, as small as two. Of these two, one took the important initial step of inviting the other.

7. *Envisioning.* Finally, there is the service of envisioning. Martin Luther King Jr.'s "I Have a Dream" speech continues to inspire after many years. The ministry on which all the others depend is the ability to see in the mind's eye that reality in which we place our hope. We do not need the eloquence of Martin Luther King Jr. to exercise this ministry. Each of us has a capacity

to envision a future of peace and justice in some detail, a future that corresponds more closely to God's preferred future for our world. Quite possibly our envisioning capacity is very underdeveloped. Although early schooling did little for many of us to awaken and train this vital capacity, it is never too late to begin.

War is an institution for which revisioning is of vital importance today. War is a human institution that has been with us so long that many people, perhaps most, think it is essential to security and that we will always have wars. The church teaches otherwise: "Divine Providence urgently demands of us that we free ourselves from the age-old slavery of war."[2] This liberation can come about only when an alternative way to provide security replaces war. This alternative will first exist as a realistic proposition in peoples' minds; it depends for its beginning on envisioning. There are many other areas where creative imagination is precisely what is needed in situations of injustice. All of us can train ourselves to appreciate the creative people among us, and especially to welcome the latent creativity within ourselves. Those who see what is still out of sight for many others have an indispensable role to play in the effort for justice and peace.

Jesus and the Seven Ways

In our prayer we can take these seven ways and reflect on them, one by one, in the life of Jesus. All seven ways can be seen in the gospel accounts of his ministry. Jesus consistently *reminded* those around him of the plight of the poor, often in dramatic ways, by healing, feeding crowds, and speaking up on behalf of those who were discounted as of little or no importance. He was ingenious in *interpreting* life from the perspective of those who were poor and suffering in any way. He *envisioned* an alternative reality that he called the reign of God, or the kingdom of God. This was his great overarching vision. This ability to envision explains, at least in part, his remarkable teaching ministry. His hearers were quick to note that "he taught them as one having authority, and not as their scribes" (Matt 7:29). While those who opposed Jesus had adjusted the law and the teaching of the prophets to their own advantage, Jesus plumbed the depths of the same law and prophets they quoted, and from those same sources, tested in prayer, drew a vision that touches the inner core of persons of every age.

Jesus was both *advocate* and *resister.* In the account of the woman taken in adultery, we see Jesus boldly resisting the scribes and pharisees in their cruel and callous attempt to use a woman to get at Jesus. At the same time he is the advocate for the woman who is victim of their cruelty. Surely what we know of Jesus testifies to his deep *caring* that so attracted people of all kinds: mothers who brought their children to be blessed, the parents of the twelve-year-old girl who was thought dead, the woman who braved the crowd to touch the hem of his cloak, and so many more. Basic to Jesus' ministry was the *foundation of a community of disciples.* The church developed from this community of men and women united by their experience of Jesus, and by their faith and love confirmed by the gift of the Holy Spirit.

In reflection on the ministry of Jesus in relationship to the joys and hopes, the griefs and anxieties of the people of our time, especially the poor, we discover day by day the very personal and urgent call of God in our own lives.[3] Our ministry will have a particular accent related to our particular gifts, talents, and character traits. In community with others we can do more than we ever thought possible when we give ourselves wholeheartedly to the vision and mission of Jesus. We will hear him saying to us, "I have called you friends, because I have made known to you everything that I have heard from my Father" (John 15:15).

Ecumenical and Interreligious Dialogue

*Only the truth that is experienced at all levels of being has
the power to change the human being.*
—Rollo May

When it issues in shared action for peace and justice, ecumenical and interreligious dialogue may be an essential way to finding a safe passage into a new world order. In many places in the world today, people profess different religious beliefs and practices that give meaning and coherence to their lives. Where dialogue is missing, negative stereotyping too often takes its place. The dialogue needed is a dialogue of life, which is not the same as academic theological discussion, though that will continue to be important as well. A dialogue of life requires sharing in a spirit of respect and trust. In such an atmosphere people can explain to one another what faith really means on a personal level, how it informs and influences their joys, hopes, struggles and sufferings, and their view of society. When people are able to share this way in small groups, their motivation and energy for the difficult work of peacemaking can be greatly strengthened. Friendships forged by sharing in this spirit can sustain difficulties that can and do otherwise tear people, communities, and societies apart.

Since the Second Vatican Council, Catholic social teaching has consistently promoted ecumenical and interreligious dialogue. Pope John XXIII, a modern pioneer in this effort, steadfastly held to two principles in this dialogue. The first was to lay stress on what people have in common. This did not deny or neglect differences, but gave first consideration to shared goals and interests. The second principle was human solidarity based on humanity's common origin and common questions about the meaning of life, and increasingly on their common interdependence, a theme of Pope John's first social encyclical, *Christianity and Social Progress* (1961) .

Pope John Paul II wrote of the importance of dialogue not only with people of other religious beliefs but also with other philosophies and cultures. Speaking of the missionary activity of the church, he wrote:

> This missionary duty, moreover, does not prevent us from approaching dialogue with an attitude of profound willingness to listen. We know in fact that, in the presence of the mystery of grace, infinitely full of possibilities and implications for human life and history, the church herself will never cease putting questions, trusting in the help of the Paraclete, the Spirit of truth (cf. John 14:17), whose task it is to guide her "into all the truth" (John 16:13).
>
> This is a fundamental principle not only for the endless theological investigation of Christian truth, but also for Christian dialogue with other philosophies, cultures, and religions. In the common experience of humanity, for all its contradictions, the Spirit of God, who "blows where he wills" (John 3:8), not infrequently reveals signs of his presence which help Christ's followers to understand more deeply the message which they bear.[4]

In his World Day of Peace message for 2001, Pope John Paul II turned again to the topic of dialogue and made reference to a meeting in Assisi in 1986 in which representatives of many religions met and prayed in each other's presence. It was a significant new way of coming together. Rather than attempt to find words of prayer that would be authentic for all, they honored each religion's way of prayer by being prayerfully present while the followers of different religions prayed. John Paul wrote, "My many encounters with representatives of other religions—I recall especially the meeting in Assisi in 1986 and in St. Peter's Square in 1999—have made me more confident that mutual openness between the followers of the various religions can greatly serve the cause of peace and the common good of the human family."[5]

Ecumenical, interreligious, and also intercultural dialogue promises to be increasingly important in peace and justice efforts. The interreligious experience in Assisi in 1986 suggests a way that local groups in many places could follow. It incorporates in prayer elements of compassionate listening and benevolent glancing discussed in chapter 3. This may be a new frontier in active nonviolence.

In the search for the meaning of life, the farthest horizon goes by various names: God, ground of being, divine mystery, or absolute future. An idea of God is not God. God is not an object we can grasp. We are closer to the truth when we discern God in giving and receiving love. As an early Christian hymn says, "Where charity and love are, there is God." Different world religions have their own ways to talk about God and eventually hand down their most important teachings in sacred texts from which we can learn something about a religious tradition's understanding of God. As valuable as these texts are, they hand on ideas about God within a tradition; they do not give us God.

To discern or experience God, more than the mind must be involved. If the texts are to have their intended meaning for us, we must recognize religious truths in our own experience, for this is how God comes to us. While our best experiences of self-transcendence speak to us of a "beyond" that is somehow not constrained by space and time, so do our painful experiences suggest powerfully that there must be some good reality beyond whatever tragedy we or others may experience. In short, we have a visceral rebellion against evil and absurdity.

Religion can provide meaning in our lives and is thus such a powerful force in society. Organized religions hand themselves on through communities of believers who develop distinctive ways of expressing their beliefs, handing on their traditions, and interacting with other groups within a society. The dictum that the corruption of the best is the worst applies in the case of religion. Religion corrupted has fueled some of the worst atrocities in history, providing misguided rationale for torture, wars, and genocide. We do not have to look to the distant past to see this demonstrated. The abuses associated with religion have led some people to have nothing to do with religion, and to attempt to live wholly secular lives. The fact that religion refuses to disappear suggests strongly that ignoring religion is not a constructive approach to dealing with it.

Today we are faced with potential for evil that was earlier unthinkable. The human race is now capable of destroying itself and the very planet as a habitation for living beings of all kinds. The danger of omnicide by nuclear, biological, or chemical warfare or a combination of these means can be lessened but never eliminated. It is not the only threat of devastating destruction. The danger of ecological damage beyond repair continues to loom large and is intimately bound up with what we call lifestyle, involving basic issues of justice and solidarity as a necessary mode of love.

If we make some immediate, fundamental changes in the course of the next few decades, we will not be doomed to destroy ourselves and to deny the possibility of life to future generations. The worst of times can also be the best of times, a time of redemption. More than ever before we have the technological possibilities for knowing and acting together in respectful and cooperative ways. These technological capabilities cannot save us; they can help us solve problems, and they can point to deeper mysteries of human responsibility where we come face to face with matters of faith, hope, and love, virtues honored by all world religions.

An understanding of what religions have in common is best sought in what we do, in how we live with one another. Here there can be much common ground. It is by living attentively, reflectively, by doing unto others as we would have them do unto us that we experience our common humanity as open to a mystery beyond the life cycle we share with other living creatures. When we try to love our neighbors as ourselves, we displace ourselves from the center of our attention. The Emmaus Community, founded in France at the end of World War II, has an insightful way of expressing this truth. After some years of effort at postwar peace building, they were able to articulate the fundamental principle at the heart of their movement: "Serve, before yourself, those less fortunate; serve first those who suffer the most." In trying to live by this principle, the Emmaus Community see service not as patronizing, but as a dynamism that puts right order into a society.

An economy based on this principle would assure that all had their needs met. To the extent that people look out for the most vulnerable as their first priority, they take care of the basic human needs of those who could otherwise be ignored. To live by the opposite of this principle, to serve first oneself, or one's nation, and then to give some aid to those who are left behind in a competitive society, guarantees that there will be a growing gap between rich and poor, with all the negative social consequences.

The principle of the Emmaus Community goes well beyond the golden rule, "Do unto others as you would have them do unto you." Christians who try to follow the teachings of Jesus are called to go beyond the golden rule; they are not to do unto others as they would have the others do unto them, but to treat others as Jesus did. "I give you a new commandment, that you love one another. Just as I have loved you, you also should love one another....This is my commandment, that you love one another as I have loved you. No one has greater love than this, to lay down one's life for one's friends" (John 13:34, 15:12–13). Jesus experienced God as letting the sun shine and rain fall on good and bad alike, a God of unconditional love calling us to universal love. By the way he lived, Jesus forged such solidarity with poor people that he aroused lethal hostility from some of those in positions of religious and political power who lived off the labor of the poor without regard for their human dignity and their basic rights that flow from that dignity. In fidelity to his unconditional love, Jesus laid down his life not only for his friends but also for those who saw themselves as his enemies. The mystery of life is here plumbed at great depth. We find life by giving it in unconditional love.

Working with Others in Organized Justice and Peace Movements

Many people, realizing that by working together they can multiply the impact an individual can have on social issues, work for justice and peace through organizations; they also benefit from the information, analysis, and moral support that they gain by belonging to an organized movement. Following are brief descriptions of a number of peace and justice organizations that exemplify Catholic social teaching and its roots in the gospel. Some are Catholic and others are ecumenical or interfaith movements.

The Catholic Worker Movement was founded by Dorothy Day and Peter Maurin in New York at the height of the Great Depression of the 1930s. The movement still provides houses of hospitality in many places in the United States and in some other countries. The two New York houses produce a paper, *The Catholic Worker*. Several other U.S. houses also produce a regular publication. The Catholic Worker is distinguished by its practice of the works of mercy and by its commitment to voluntary poverty and nonviolence inspired by the gospel. (www.catholicworker.org)

Pax Christi International, founded in 1945 in France, is a federation of national sections of the movement and affiliated groups in more than thirty countries. Its purpose is to work for peace for all people, always witnessing to the peace of Christ through prayer, study, and action. Pax Christi USA began in 1972. The membership is largely lay, but includes religious, priests, and bishops. Pax Christi is open to all who agree with its mission. Recognizing that peace is the fruit of justice, Pax Christi is as much a justice movement as a peace movement. It fosters a Christian spirituality that expresses itself in action for justice and peace. (www.paxchristi.net and www.paxchristiusa.org)

The American Fellowship of Reconciliation (FOR), the oldest interfaith peace organization in the United States, was founded in 1915. It is the largest section of the International Fellowship of Reconciliation founded in Europe a year earlier. FOR is avowedly pacifist, that is, its members refuse any cooperation with war or its preparation. The thrust of FOR's activities is on the promotion of active nonviolence, that is, the use of powers of love and truth to address violence, including the violence of unjust economic and social institutions. (www.forusa.org)

Since its beginning in 1971, *Network,* a national lobbying organization, has earned respect and praise among members of the U.S. Congress for its careful analysis of issues and its principled response. Network was founded by Catholic Sisters as a direct response to Pope Paul VI's apostolic letter, *A Call to Action.* The staff of the organization analyzes issues that are before Congress and then educates its members on selected national and international issues in the light of Catholic social teaching. Network is a membership organization that alerts its members when citizen lobbying is needed on a particular issue. Network also publishes educational materials and offers workshops to teach effective citizen lobbying. (www.networklobby.org)

Center of Concern, founded in 1971, promotes social analysis, theological reflection, policy advocacy, and public education on issues of global development, domestic/global links, trade, economic justice, and human rights. The Center's bimonthly publication, *Center Focus,* informs and educates on all these issues. (www.coc.org)

Bread for the World, an ecumenical citizens' lobby, focuses on world hunger and effective ways of working against it as a matter of justice. Founded in 1974, Bread for the World supplies its members with analyses of national and international hunger-related issues as matters of human rights, and specifically of the right to food. Members are urged to do their work in the context of Bible study and worship. (www.bread.org)

Three justice and peace organizations that report directly to the United States Conference of Catholic Bishops are the Campaign for Human Development, Catholic Relief Services, and Catholic Charities. The *Campaign for Human Development* (CHD; www.povertyusa.org) awards grants for social and economic development projects in the United States that empower poor people to direct them. *Catholic Relief Services* (CRS; www.catholicrelief.org) is the U.S. church's overseas humanitarian relief and development agency, founded during World War II and now working throughout the world. Expert in disaster relief, CRS is also a very effective development agency helping poor people in many countries in local development projects. CRS also develops educational programs and materials to help American Catholics understand international justice and peace issues and constructive ways of address-ing them. *Catholic Charities* (www.catholiccharities.org) is organ-ized on the diocesan level and is a major U.S. agency in the field of social welfare. On the national level it is a strong advocate for adequate welfare legislation.

The *Interfaith Center on Corporate Responsibility* (ICCR) is an international coalition of 275 faith-based institutional investors including denominations, religious communities, pension funds, health care corporations, foundations, and dioceses with com-bined portfolios worth an estimated $100 billion. As responsible stewards, they merge social values with investment decisions, believing they must achieve more than an acceptable financial return. ICCR members utilize religious investments and other resources to change unjust or harmful corporate policies, and in this way they work for peace, economic justice, and stewardship of the Earth. (www.iccr.org)

Some organized movements have a sharp focus on a particu-lar area of social justice. *Interfaith Worker Justice* (www.nicwj.org) is an ecumenical organization that works to educate, organize, and mobilize the religious community in the United States on issues and campaigns that will improve wages, benefits, and working conditions for workers, especially low-wage workers. The *United Farm Workers* (www.ufw.org) continue the work begun under the leadership of Cesar Chavez, advocating for justice for agricultural farm workers who include many migrant workers. *Global Peace Services-USA* (www.globalpeaceservices.org) is a membership organization that promotes educational programs to equip people to use methods of active nonviolence in dealing with violence and conflict at all levels.

Creativity and Stability

Each of these organized movements is characterized by a shared vision of the possibility of a more just and peaceful world. By its very nature, social justice and peace work brings together people who share beliefs, values, and concerns. They soon dis-cover that by mutual support they can make a difference. At times, in response to a keenly felt issue, these movements attract many participants and succeed in bringing about change in the short run. For the long haul, the belief in the possibility of a better world gives movements coherence and keeps them alive despite external obstacles and the limitations of the members.

In order to stay with an issue or a vision of a preferred future for a long time, movements develop a stable organization of some kind. This has both assets and challenges. From her long experience with peace movements, sociologist Elise Boulding has written of the inherent tension between movement and organization:

> There is a core element of social excitement in the very concept of peace *movement.* Deep feelings about human oneness surge forward, and people are mobilized for action. But without social forms in which to express the oneness, the feelings fade away. The paradox is that social forms, i.e. peace organizations themselves, depend on continued fresh infusions of enthusiasms, yet the very demands of organizational activity dull the vibrancy of intention.[6]

The demands of organizational activity need not "dull the vibrancy of intention." Organized justice and peace movements keep vibrant intention and a clear focus alive when they include in their strategies ways to return regularly to the spiritual sources from which they are fed. Such movements become strong while others tend to fade away as issues change. Put another way, peace and justice organizations, like individuals, flourish as they are attentive, understanding, reasonable, and responsible, held by "the love that moves the sun and the other stars."[7]

QUESTIONS FOR STUDY, REFLECTION, AND CONVERSATION

1. Of the seven ways of working for justice and peace described in this chapter, which ones appeal most strongly to you? Why? Can you think of other ways?

2. Prayer is not listed among the seven ways. Can you think of a reason for this omission? How do you see the relationship between prayer and action?

3. Do you find that your preferred ways of working have changed at different times of your life? What are some of the factors that account for this?

4. Do you know others who work in ways other than your preferred way? Does a consideration of the seven ways help you to a deeper appreciation of their work and of your own?

5. What does a consideration of Jesus and the seven ways contribute to your understanding? To your motivation?

6. Have you experienced ecumenical or interfaith dialogue? If so, what were its benefits? Its challenges? Its potential? Why is it more important than ever?

7. What has been your experience in working within justice and peace movements and organizations? Why are they important?

8. How do you deal with the impossibility of responding to all the requests that come from organizations that work to help others? Do you have a standard? A rule of thumb?

9. Do you consider contributions other than monetary, for example, volunteering time? Participating in activities of the organization?

10. If you are using this book with a class or group, consider asking different members to find out more about the movements and organizations described in this chapter, and share the information.

NOTES

1. See chapter 4, section on "Nonviolence and Hospitality," pages 49–50.

2. *Gaudium et Spes,* art. 81, p. 223, in David J. O'Brien and Thomas A. Shannon, eds., *Catholic Social Thought: The Documentary Heritage* (Maryknoll, NY: Orbis, 1992).

3. Ibid., art. 1, p. 166.

4. Pope John Paul II, Apostolic Letter, *"Novo Millenio Ineunte,"* *Origins* 30 (31): January 18, 2001, 506.

5. Pope John Paul II, World Day of Peace Message 2001, "Dialogue between Cultures for a Civilization of Love and Peace," art. 16, *Origins* 30(29): January 4, 2001, 462.

6. Elise Boulding, *Cultures of Peace: The Hidden Side of History* (Syracuse, NY: Syracuse University Press, 2000), 84.

7. Dante Alighieri, *The Divine Comedy,* Canto thirty-three (New York: Penquin Books, 1984), 347.